Lights & Sirens

BEHIND THE SCENES

Lights & Sirens

A writer's guide to emergency response teams

James & Lois Cowan

WRITER'S DIGEST BOOKS
CINCINNATI, OHIO

Lights & Sirens. Copyright © 1998 by James and Lois Cowan. Manufactured in the United States of America. All rights reserved. No part of this book may be reproduced in any form or by any electronic or mechanical means including information storage and retrieval systems without permission in writing from the publisher, except by a reviewer, who may quote brief passages in a review. Published by Writer's Digest Books, an imprint of F&W Publications, Inc., 1507 Dana Avenue, Cincinnati, Ohio 45207. (800) 289-0963. First edition.

Other fine Writer's Digest Books are available from your local bookstore or direct from the publisher.

02   01   00   99   98   5   4   3   2   1

Library of Congress Cataloging-in-Publication Data
Cowan, James
    Lights & sirens / James and Lois Cowan.
        p.   cm.—(Behind the scenes)
    Includes bibliographical references and index.
    ISBN 0-89879-806-X (pbk.: alk. paper)
    1. Emergency medical services. 2. Rescue work. 3. Emergency medical
technicians. I. Cowan, Lois. II. Title. III. Title: Lights and sirens IV. Series.
RA645.5.C69   1998
362.18—dc21   97-48735
                                                                                CIP

Edited by Jack Heffron
Production edited by Michelle Kramer
Interior designed by Sandy Kent
Cover designed by Stephanie Redman

Photos on pages 14, 64, 178 and 208 are © CMC Rescue, Inc., used by permission.

About the Authors

Lois and James (Terry) Cowan are a writing team and emergency rescue partners. Their works include over a dozen fiction and non-fiction books, plus articles for children and adults focusing on pre-hospital emergency medicine. They are members of the Mystery Writers of America and the National Writers Union. Active in the statewide Wilderness Rescue Team with specialties in swiftwater, high-angle rescue and wilderness medicine, and holding post-graduate degrees from Harvard and Goddard College, both were EMTs and are paramedics with experience in urban and rural settings. They are NASAR certified in "Managing the Lost Person Incident." Lois Cowan is president of the Maine Paramedic Association. Terry Cowan, a firefighter, is a regional EMS director, associate EMS director and education coordinator of his service, and a state-certified EMS instructor/coordinator. Both work as consultants for EMS-legal issues.

Parents of eight children and two grandchildren, they and their horses live on a saltwater spread, TLC Farm, on a midcoast Maine island.

Acknowledgments

The editor of *Lights and Sirens* would like to thank the following people for their help in making this book as accurate and useful as possible:

Captain Mark Wagner, Green Township Fire Department, rescue expert extraordinaire

Harvey Eisner from:
Firehouse Magazine
PTN Publishing
445 Broad Hollow Rd., Suite 21
Melville, NY 11747
Tel: 516/845-2700
Fax: 516/845-7109

Kimberly Bird and Tammy Wells from:
Ferno-Washington, Inc.
70 Weil Way
Wilmington, OH 45177
800/733-3766

Harold Haider at:
CMC Rescue, Inc.
PO Drawer 6870
Santa Barbara, CA 93160-6870
USA Customer Service
Tel: 800/235-5741
Fax: 800/235-8951
International Customer Service
Tel: 805/967-3575
Fax: 805/967-8951
Customerservice@cmcrescue.com
http://www.cmcrescue.com

For Brendan and Nina,
following old paths to new destinations

| TABLE OF CONTENTS |

The World of Rescue

Rescue is a little-understood activity. It has been popularized by television, movies and novels, but rarely is emergency response depicted realistically and accurately. We hope to change this situation by offering you, the writer, help in researching the information you need to "get it right."

Once you understand rescue and are comfortable describing it, you've opened a whole new world to your characters—a world of stress, challenge, interaction and adventure, usually with some blood and gore thrown in. It is a sphere that focuses on people in real or threatened distress. The need for rescue can arise whenever you wish, day or night; in the home or workplace; on land, in water or in the air; in urban, rural or wilderness settings.

We are a husband-and-wife medic team, search-and-rescue partners and coauthors who aim to give you the knowledge you need to integrate rescuers and rescues into your works. We have organized our information about the sixteen distinct professions under the rescue rubric within the *LAST* framework: *Locate/Access/Stabilize/Treat*. No doubt this is the order your story will follow after your character gets into a mess in the first place. The following chart provides a quick overview of the rescue roles within the LAST framework.

The *L* in LAST—*Locate*—is the first step. Find the victim, whether lost in the woods or lying in the hallway with a fractured

Types of Rescuers

Those Who Locate

DISPATCHER

Skills

Sits at console, answers phones, sends out personnel and equipment. Speaks coherently; thinks on feet; needs interpersonal skills. Dispatch runs show at the beginning. Must know resources and when to call for more. Higher-trained dispatchers or telecommunicators give prearrival instructions.

Education

Certification programs available. Many parts of the country—in particular rural regions—do not require certification or formal training. Basic dispatching courses run about forty hours.

Notes

Computer-assisted dispatch (CAD) uses monitor and software to record rescue information. Emergency medical dispatch (EMD) utilizes guide cards or computer software to help deal with emergency until rescuers arrive. You should describe both systems as prioritizing responses.

SEARCHER

Skills

Organizational skills include turning out and managing volunteers. Familiar with local terrain and resources. Formal search training and experience helpful but not commonly found. Actual searchers need enthusiasm, proper gear, map and compass skills.

Education

National Association for Search and Rescue (NASAR) certification in "Fundamentals of Search and Rescue" (FUNSAR). State or local course equivalents.

Notes

Depending upon the outcome you desire, include in your writings those trained, those at least organized and those disorganized and dangerous to themselves and the search.

DOG HANDLER

Skills

Agility; enthusiasm; love of canines. Dedication to a lifelong self-education program and constant reinforcement-training for the dog and handler. Must be able to read maps, orienteer and debrief to search manager.

Education

NASAR is working with search-and-rescue (SAR) dog organizations to develop a national certification. In the meantime, regional and team standards include agility, obedience and tracking skills.

Notes

In your well-organized search, your SAR dog units should be first in the field before scent and tracks are destroyed by other searchers. A unit—dog and handler—works alone in a defined search sector.

RANGER

Skills

Rangers are skilled in the use of firearms. They are outdoor people who must get along with campers and tourists. They are often cross-trained in other rescue professions: technical, water, winter.

Education

College degree. Law enforcement training. Certification in cardiopulmonary resuscitation (CPR). "Managing the Search Function" and Incident Command System (ICS) training. Emergency Medical Services (EMS) licensure is highly prized.

Notes

Rangers are frequently the pros who put the ICS into play when a person is lost. When your story includes a major search, call in the rangers to establish and man the ICS.

Those Who Access

FIREFIGHTER

Skills

Those suffering from rescue syndrome—a need to be a hero—do not last long. Firefighters (ffs) follow their superior's orders and work well with other rescue professionals. More frequently there are physical standards they must meet in terms of endurance and strength.

Education

Local, regional and national fire attack schools teach the use of self-contained breathing apparatus (SCBA) and search techniques. Many firefighters are cross-trained as emergency medical technicians (EMTs). This allows your character to perceive the victim as a patient from the moment of rescue.

Notes

While ffs are most commonly depicted running from a burning building with a saved child in their arms, you'd be more accurate making your hero specialized. Your ff, whose job it is to access, might arrive separately from the other fire responders on a special rescue truck. Her concern will not be the preservation of property, but of lives.

EXTRICATION SPECIALIST

Skills

These technicians are tool heads. Their expertise lies in an understanding of the mechanics and construction of vehicles and structures, and in the use of hydraulic tools. They will have an innate understanding of physics, and will know what happens if something is moved, bent, cut or twisted.

Education

Extricationists have annual competitions that include continuing education. Fire schools and commercial educators offer courses in extrication. Often tool manufacturers will demonstrate their product and include hands-on experience. The classrooms for the extrication specialists are the wrecked buildings and auto scrap yards.

Notes

When push comes to shove, your professional rescuers should stand back while the extrication team goes to work. Their knowledge is respected; they are the ones counted on to assure a safe scene and provide access to victims.

Types of Rescuers, continued

Those Who Access, continued

HAZMAT RESPONDER

Skills

This responder has been trained to understand hazardous material (hazmat) codes, identification numbers, chemicals and their reactions. She has medical knowledge as it pertains to hazmat exposure. Because the air in a confined space is compromised, your hazmat responder can efficiently deal with these rescues as well.

Education

The hazmat rescuer will have a thorough understanding of the protective gear she must wear. She will be able to work efficiently within those restraints. She will be SCBA-certified and trained in blind location orientation.

Notes

Like the firefighter, the hazmat responder's workplace is an environment not fit for humans. For the hazmat expert, the dangers are invisible and insidious.

WATER RESCUER

Skills

Rescue swimmers, rescue divers, swift-water rescuers and open water responders all understand the power of their foe. All will be expert swimmers. Depending upon their venue, they will be knowledgeable about boats and helicopters (helos), technical rope work and ice rescue.

Education

All types of water responders will be certified in CPR. River runners dealing with white water will have training as swiftwater technicians. Underwater rescuers will have dive cetifications. All will have first aid; many will be EMTs.

Notes

Be sure you know the environment you place your water rescuer in. Different kinds of water present vastly different problems and chances for rescue.

ROPE RESCUER

Skills

This rescuer will be a technical climbing specialist with years of experience probably all over the planet. He will know his equipment and trust his life—and the subject he is rescuing—on it. This is not a field entered lightly. These athletes are seasoned professionals.

Education

While there are schools for technical climbers and commercial indoor climbing walls on which to practice these skills, those who rescue have learned through thousands of hours of rock-climbing experience on their own.

Notes

Of all the rescuers available for you to write about, the rope rescuer is the most attractive. Their rope, their outfits and their lifestyles are colorful.

WINTER RESCUER

Skills

Winter rescuers must be able to take care of themselves in extreme conditions, and must understand the insidiousness and tenacity of cold. They will be skilled at snowshoeing, skiing, rafting, hiking and ice climbing. They will be expert orienteers.

Education

Formal education is not the prerequisite this pro follows. This is practical training in the field. Experience is the winter rescuer's best teacher. Ski patrollers will have completed a course that includes basic wilderness first responder (WFR) medical skills. These folks are referred to as wofers.

Notes

This rescuer's expertise is dependent upon equipment simply to be able to reach the victim. In addition, the gear necessary to bring the subject back is extensive. Build your winter rescuers with strong backs.

CAVE RESCUER

Skills

A complete lack of claustrophobia is essential. Cave rescuers are experienced and innovative problem solvers. Rarely do they deal with the same dilemma twice. These men and women will be agile, and able to twist and turn as they help the subject out of his hole, jam or crack.

Education

Cave rescuers take rope rigging and vertical and high-angle rescue courses offered by independent educators and fire departments. Cave rescue often overlaps with other specialities such as confined space, extrication and trench rescue. The pro will be cross-trained. Few areas will have enough cave emergencies to support cave rescuers exclusively.

Notes

Remember that spelunkers now have decided they wish to be called cavers.

SEARCH-AND-RESCUE TEAM

Skills

Urban and wilderness professional searchers use the same techniques, modified for their particular environments. They will have training in all of the various search techniques. NASAR and the National Association of Urban Search and Rescue both offer courses and certification.

Education

Urban SAR teams will be well-versed in extrication as they deal with collapsed structures. Both types of searchers need an excellent sense of direction, acute hearing and vision. They must be in good physical shape. They need to be available when called out.

Notes

In addition to search techniques, these rescuers will be competent at short hauls, hot landings and helo rescue techniques. When your imaginary subjects are finally located, these are the pros who must access and get them out of their present situation.

Types of Rescuers, continued

Those Who Stabilize

FIRST RESPONDER

Skills

First Responders (FRs) are capable of first aid-level care to keep the patient stable until EMS professionals in the form of EMTs and medics are on the scene. In some areas, firefighters trained as first responders answer 911 calls from neighborhood stations sooner than higher-level EMTs and medics, who travel from more centralized locations.

Education

Some firefighters (ffs) are cross-trained as paramedics. More commonly, the ff who is a first responder has about twenty-five hours of training including about eight hours of CPR instruction. The FR is a certified and licensed EMS responder in most states and regions. (Frequently, the firefighter-FR is not an EMS-licensed provider, but has been designated a FR through minimal CPR training and Red Cross-like first aid instruction.)

Notes

FRs have different roles in urban and rural areas. Where there is a shortage of EMS responders, first responders take a greater role in medical care.

EMERGENCY MEDICAL TECHNICIAN

Skills

This is the first EMS level to both treat and transport. EMTs supervise FRs and provide basic life support (BLS) at the medical or trauma scene. They prioritize problems, initiate treatment and communicate by radio.

Education

In addition to maintaining a professional rescuer-level CPR certification, basic EMTs endure 400 hours of didactic and practical education. Some states have advanced life support (ALS) EMTs who, after 110 additional hours of training, establish IVs and perform other invasive (entering the body) procedures.

Notes

EMTs are inaccurately depicted in literature. Don't you dare call your hardworking EMT an ambulance attendant! They are medical professionals who deal daily with life-and-death situations.

Those Who Treat

PARAMEDIC

Skills

1,500 hours above EMT-Basic, paramedic training includes an on-ambulance internship and in-hospital medical education in the emergency department, burn, surgical and intensive care units, IV therapy department, pediatrics, obstetrics, psychology and coronary care.

Education

Certification is proof of education; licensure is granted by individual states. Paramedics and EMTs are the only medical providers who must relicense—with proof of continuing medical education (CME)—every 2 to 3 years, depending upon a particular state's requirements.

Notes

Outside of the hospital, your medic is the highest licensed, best-trained medical provider to save your character's life, or to take charge of a bloody scene your villain has created. Unless the only treatment is a surgical suite, she will treat on-scene rather than rush to the hospital.

6

Rescue can be a frustrating and dangerous experience, but often it is a rewarding one too. This firefighter returns a dog to its grateful owner after rescuing it from a burning building. (Photo used by permission of Harvey Eisner.)

hip. This might involve helicopters, dogs, grid searchers or a 911 emergency medical services (EMS) response.

Once a victim is found, it may be necessary to get him out of the fix he's gotten himself into—whether that means getting him off a cliff, out from under an overturned semi or up from the bathroom floor. This is *A—Access*. Access can be two-tiered as we say in rescue. First, it might involve creating a safe approach to the victim, such as shoring up with cribbing a flipped tractor. Next, the tractor's jammed door might need to be cut away. Then, in an inherently unsafe setting, access might entail moving the victim out of harm's way and to a place where more help can be provided. For example, it is prudent to move the farmer away from the spilled gasoline pooling in the ditch that the tractor slid into. All such actions are part of the access scenario.

If the now located and accessed subject is injured, he becomes a patient and the rescuers' immediate goal is to *Stabilize* him—the *S* in LAST. This involves getting him to the point where his medical condition will not deteriorate.

Paramedics will *Treat*—the *T* in LAST. Only EMS providers are trained to practice out-of-hospital emergency medicine. Most life-saving invasive procedures that books describe emergency physicians performing are, in fact, accomplished by medics in the woods, on the edge of interstates, in squalid tenements, under poor lighting and with no assistants. It is an unforgiving environment for surgical procedures, initiation of IV therapy and administration of powerful drugs.

If medics are not on-scene, certain advanced treatments may be forestalled until the patient arrives at the hospital, although emergency medical technicians (EMTs) are skilled at some of the same emergency procedures as hospital personnel and medics.

But it all begins out there in the middle of a riot, in the avalanche or in the midst of a domestic disturbance, which, incidentally, is not going to be the safest spot for your protagonist. What tends to save the situation is teamwork.

In unstable, dangerous settings, teamwork is the glue that holds the operation together. This is particularly interesting because the common characteristic of the rescue professional is an independent, cocky spirit overlaid with a desire to live on the edge. This is not the personality type one conjures up when thinking of a team player. Yet the rescuer is frequently part of a larger effort. The victim is not necessarily found in a viable condition, but the team, which does all it can do given the circumstances, is organized and cohesive.

To understand and be able to write about how such ad hoc teams mesh, you need familiarity with the various rescue vocations and how their unique roles and responsibilities intertwine. Then you can deftly weave them together to satisfy your saga's needs.

As a writer, your credibility is lost at great peril to the story line. That is, the firefighter who reads your description of her work will lose faith in your whole novel if you've got her wearing the wrong pants and holding incorrectly described gear. This behind the scenes book will allow you to place your ranger, cave rescuer, telecommunicator or search dog-handler in rescue situations—accurately, believably and comfortably.

The Incident Command System

It used to be that when there was an emergency, a community looked for help to a local physician, a handy neighbor familiar with the particular problem or whomever else could be gathered together. But in our complex society, where we are no longer used to or even capable of solving our own problems, professionals have filled the gap.

Think about it. There is a considerable difference between these two scenarios: pulling the driver from a Model A; and extricating victims of a mass casualty incident (MCI) in which a semi has careened off an overpass onto three cars, which were then blindsided by a loaded school bus that ended up rolling over.

Under the auspices of local or regional fire departments, rescue teams were formed. But there was too much to know and too much change for everyone to keep current. As a result, rescue specialties were formed, ready to work together.

These team members frequently meet for the first time at the emergency site. But all should be well-versed in a system used throughout the United States: the Incident Command System

(ICS). ICS was devised to manage just such a mix of strangers, each with her own rescue agenda. You can get involved in a mass casualty incident in California, Ohio and Florida, and everyone will follow the same organizational plan and doing the same drill. ICS comes into play whenever an event outstrips local, available resources, either because of the time factor, number of victims, logistics, or lack of equipment or personnel. This plan handles every aspect of an incident.

Look at the ICS chart on page 12. Although it is geared to searches, the system is so generic that it easily converts for use with an explosion, train wreck or nuclear plant disaster. This structure was first implemented by fire services and is now used by virtually all emergency responders throughout the country including police, fire, EMS and search-and-rescues (SAR). It is applicable to any incident that locally available resources cannot handle. The beauty is that people trained in particular roles can play out those roles no matter what the incident. It is predicated upon the administrative notion that control is kept as long as no more than five personnel report to a higher-level person.

A component of ICS deals with the day-to-day needs of the rescuers as well as the rescue objective. Even as search teams comb the mountainous terrain for the lost family and the temperature dips ten degrees with the setting sun, rescuers need to eat, sleep and keep warm and dry.

It seems obvious that making youself a victim along with the primary subject is counterproductive. That's why heroics are frowned upon by professional rescuers. Question #1 always is, "Is the scene safe for me?" Everyone gets grumpy when a rescuer puts herself at peril and loses. Dragging two injured people through snow fields is a lot harder than dealing with one. And when the media praises such an individual who is in rare cases successful, thousands of professional rescuers feel disgust. It isn't *professional* to place yourself in danger and then have your colleagues—your teammates—bail you out. There's enough inherent danger in rescue without creating more or adding unnecessary risks.

Nine times out of ten, though, rescuers act responsibly, do what they are trained to do and work side by side toward a common goal.

Those unable to set aside large egos don't tend to last long in this business.

For you to be able to describe the work and mental status of the crews and their team approach, you must know the individual players.

We're pleased to have the opportunity to introduce you—and, through you, millions of your readers—to people who have some of the most intense, dynamic, disappointing, poorly paid and fulfilling jobs in the country.

INCIDENT COMMAND SYSTEM (ICS)

This typical ICS overhead team construction (used by Maine's Warden Service) ensures that no more than five personnel ever report to one individual.

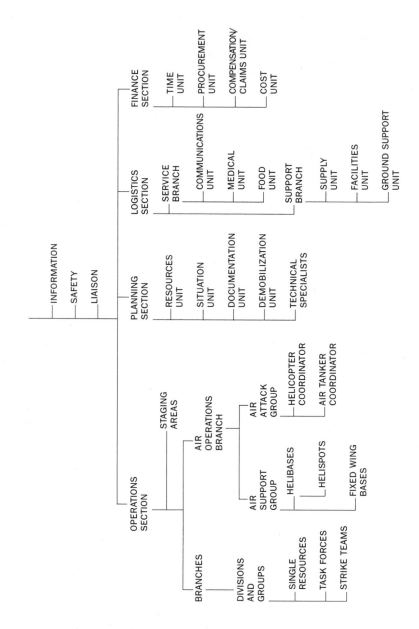

Those Who Locate

CHAPTER ONE

Dispatcher

Dispatchers—who wish the public and rescue pros would refer to them by the more professional label "telecommunicator"—practice rescue via remote control, dealing with people they cannot see. Even the caller that the dispatcher speaks with is often once removed from the victim. At its worst, dispatching is like the children's game where a whispered phrase is passed around a circle and changes to the point of hilarity. At its best, dispatching receives and transmits information, allocates resources and monitors progress with speed and accuracy.

Dispatching must be available twenty-four hours a day, 365 days a year. Like many positions, those sitting in the dispatcher's chair can be working either part time or full time. Because rural dispatchers deal with only a couple of emergencies in each twenty-four-hour period, they often work out of their homes and may run private dispatch and radio repair businesses on the side. They provide this service under contract with the town. In larger municipalities and as more centralized fire facilities replace neighborhood fire stations, dispatch is more consolidated. Modern dispatch centers are often sited to overlook the rescue vehicles and street access so the telecommunicator is able to visually monitor rescue vehicle traffic and personnel movement.

Literature tends to ignore the existence of the dispatcher, portraying rescuers directly talking to one another. In fact, that sort of radio conversation is rare. Communication is through the dispatcher, who keeps his finger on activity throughout his catchment area. Once a rescue is in progress, dispatch is the umbilicus connecting resources and advice to field responders.

A calm, assured dispatcher relaying information, responding to requests and anticipating field needs has a stabilizing influence on all rescue activities. The excellent dispatcher is an indispensable rescue professional.

History of the Profession

The earliest emergency communications were conducted by smoke signals, flags, trumpets and shouted voices. Emergency alerts were slow and inefficient. A loud "Help!" conveyed little insight into the problem at hand.

The advent of telephones and radio speeded up the initial contacts and increased information that could be conveyed. Response times to the rescue scene dropped. This was the birth of the dispatcher we know today. His ability to call out various resources created the first effective response to emergencies. And everybody discovered the obvious: Time saves lives, whether the victim is dangling from the face of a cliff or is stuck in a sewer conduit.

But nothing could transpire any more speedily than the dispatcher's ability to write or type. Every time he answered the phone or had a conversation with a rescuer in the field, he had to write it down and document it in a notebook. As he logged in his conversations with both the public and the responders, he was describing each incident step-by-step, including the times for each contact and conversation. It was tedious work.

Voice-activated tape recorders were the next logical improvement. They freed dispatchers to concentrate on the rescue process rather than function as scribes.

As the flow of information increased, it highlighted the last remaining stumbling block to efficient, modern telecommunications: the dispatchers themselves. The human element became important. A good dispatcher could make field activities work smoothly; a disorganized thinker sitting at the dispatch desk could add hours to any rescue.

The earliest dispatchers were police or firefighters nearing retirement or put on the shelf by job-related injuries. It was not a big strain to sit at a desk in the police or fire station and answer the phone, perhaps in between other clerical duties. Citizens called in with problems, and dispatch scratched down addresses and names. The responding patrol car or engine was then handed a slip of paper with that information and off they went, not knowing the details or dimensions of the problem and not sure of what to expect.

This system worked as long as there was one emergency call at a time and the dispatcher was careful to distinguish between, say, Beach and Peach Streets when he sent out responders. But by the 1960s, two to four calls were coming in at once. A dispatcher could be talking to a lady about a cat stuck in a tree while at the same time dispatching police units to a robbery in progress and a medical responder to the bystander with a heart attack. Increasing urbanization, social chaos and dependency began to overwhelm the system. So state and federal governments were forced to step in with funds and incentives for updated equipment and new training. The National Emergency Number Association's notion of a rapid response 911 phone line— the "One nation, one number" concept—was brilliant in its simplicity, and the effort was started to implement it.

In the 1980s, the first nationally based dispatch education programs appeared. Check sheets, caller ID programs and flip card systems were developed to accompany training and practice in urban systems. Computer-assisted dispatch (CAD) raised speed another notch and increased the flow of information as it linked into Enhanced 911 (E911) systems.

Dispatchers, who had been little more than public safety clerks, were taught to elicit specific, important pieces of information. *Forty-three year old male . . . a high speed car crash . . . nonresponsive but breathing . . . at the intersection of Standish and Priscilla Roads. . . .*

Through all of this, dispatchers were to keep in touch with the respondent, maintaining the connection through phone and radio from the scene to responding vehicles and receiving and relaying new information as it came in.

The next step after collecting information was to use it. "My baby's fingers are turning blue. What can I do?" Dispatchers, now carrying weighty responsibility for outcomes, were metamorphosing into telecommunicators or, when dispatching EMS, were acting as emergency medical dispatchers (EMD). With a set of rules to guide them including specific questions to get answered, they were cautioned against freelance questioning unless it enhanced, not re-placed, the protocol questions.

These treatment protocols—conversational scripts giving step-by-step prearrival instructions in life-threatening situations—al-lowed dispatchers to become remote care providers. They taught cardiopulmonary resuscitation (CPR) over the phone. They learned how to talk down the suicidal, occupying their thoughts. In fire scenes, these New Age telecommunicators would now advise their callers to stay down to avoid smoke inhalation, to place wet towels over their mouths and to feel the doors before opening them. And in hundreds of other settings, they began to convey prearrival instructions.

Today the dispatcher has joined the ranks of the professional rescuer, assuming an essential role. In fact, in most emergencies it is the dispatcher who runs the scene for the first few critical minutes, deciphering the nature and priority of the call, deciding what re-sources to send and how to get them there, all the while staying in direct contact with the voice at the other end.

Some telecommunicators dispatch for urban fire, police and EMS. Other big city dispatchers might be responsible for communi-cations of a single entity, like the City of Pittsburgh EMS. In either case, the modern job is going to include turfing calls to the appro-priate entity, such as EMS, fire, water rescue or some other branch of response. Urban systems work both ways: Some have separate dispatch for police, fire and others, while some have one center to deal with communications for several responses.

There is a clear trend, however, toward regionalism. Smaller towns and counties are pooling their resources and forming larger Public Safety Access Points or PSAPS (pronounced *Pee-saps*), which are the hub of the E911 system.

Today's state-of-the-art dispatch has picked up enough speed that the dispatch community's emphasis is turning toward quality control—doing it right the first time—rather than doing it even faster. Now telecommunicators continually evaluate emergency status, decide upon the appropriate resources and allocate manpower, all in less than sixty seconds. At the same time, he must attempt to calm the distraught

When Your Character Calls 911

There's a 911 story you might be able to integrate into your writing. In a section of the country utilizing the supercomputerized, enhanced version of the 911 system (E911), a problem developed. Frantic callers were dialing E, which is the number 3, before the 911. Then they'd sit there—having dialed 3911 rather than 911—hold the handset to their ear and wait, when in fact they had not made a connection at all. In some areas, E911 has been renamed 911E for that reason. (Dialing a 3 after 911 does not affect the connection.) The more sophisticated 911 systems are generally found in metro areas; rural settings are a bit behind because of funding and because needs are fewer. There, emergency calls are made using an 800 number or a regular seven-digit number.

Regardless of how your protagonist reached dispatch, your caller might connect with a dispatcher who types into a computer what you say and the actions taken. He will also record times. Response times are important in terms of state laws and lawsuits.

In a more cosmopolitan setting, the system before the telecommunicator might be a series of color-coded flip cards, either loaded into the computer or sitting on a desk. If the caller says, for example, "My husband says his chest hurts," the telecommunicator uses the key word CHEST PAIN, follows the prompts and works down the cardiac protocol. The answers he gets will direct him to provide a certain level of care if it is available.

The cutting edge 911 systems, called E911 or 911E, are automated. When a call comes in, the phone location, directions and appropriate jurisdiction responses to that address are on-screen. This is called ANI for automated number identification, and ALI for automated location identification. A card system will also be online. These fully computerized systems are called CAD for computer-assisted dispatch. Today, every major metropolitan area in North America provides Enhanced 911, with ALI and ANI soon available for mobile phones as well.

You can accurately mix-and-match, depending upon your story line needs. For example, a system might have a rural dispatch room and also utilize CAD or at least a card system for medical dispatch.

caller. Because these various tasks are conducted in short bursts, the stress factor is high and the potential for error is great.

Education and Certification

Thirty-two- to forty-hour dispatching courses cover dispatch systems and equipment as well as dispatching and communication skills. The most widespread training programs are run by the companies marketing dispatching hardware and software. Certification of trained dispatchers is offered by the manufacturers. For example, Salt Lake City's Medical Priority Consultants sells stand-alone card sets that are also offered as software for CAD systems. MPCs, "Emergency Medical Dispatch" and "Advanced Medical Priority Dispatch" course offerings include:

- patient care chain
- medical interrogation techniques
- medical dispatch danger zones
- chief complaint categories
- priority symptoms
- prearrival instructions
- scenario drills
- traumatic incidents
- history of EMD
- dispatch life support psychology
- negligence: the plaintiff's allegation
- risk management
- protocol principles
- time-life priority
- proven truth about EMD
- lay terminology
- reasons for EMD interrogation
- teamwork in EMS

The didactic work is informative, but a dispatcher still needs to master the art of dispatch on the job. It is an initiation by fire where a dispatcher learns best from experience and mistakes. It's axiomatic that the dispatcher's worst call comes on his first day. We know a dispatcher whose first 911 call reported a gunman holding an elementary school hostage, unknown number of teachers and students down.

Although a dispatcher sits alone with only voice contact with other rescuers, he is part of the system. In all rescue professions, training emphasizes the importance of teamwork.

Qualifications

There is no such thing as a disorganized dispatcher with job security. These men and women don't tend to be shy either, although it is not uncommon to find an introspective dispatcher who seems to put on a new, aggressive personality when he goes to work at a console and takes control, all the while remaining nameless and faceless.

He becomes a part of the rescue team as disparate individuals and agencies come together in a coordinated rescue. He is the voice and brains. If he does not stay on top of the action, he can create havoc.

The dispatcher needs to be comfortable with computerized systems and must be a rapid keyboarder who can carry on a conversation at the same time he is typing.

The dispatcher must enunciate. A mumbler would certainly create problems. There's a story about a dispatcher whose stuttering was only uncovered the first time a serious emergency was called in. However, monotones do fine as telecommunicators. A dispatcher has to accurately convey conversations between one rescuer and another when the rescuers are out of radio contact with each other, but all can speak to and hear the dispatcher with his more powerful transmitter and receiver.

When in the midst of a rescue, the dispatcher must remain calm and unfrazzled. An impatient dispatcher constantly on the air insisting upon information would destroy the rescue. He needs to understand that everyone in the field is busy and it is not necessarily convenient to take a hand away from lowering a rescuer into a confined space to respond to a dispatcher. He must sit, biting his fingernails, and wait. But not for too long! He can ask rescuers for a radio check to assure there is continuing radio contact, and probably just to calm his own nerves.

He must think on his feet for he never knows what is going to happen next. At the same time, he must follow the progress of the rescue, anticipating needs before they arise and putting backup crews on call before the request for more troops is made.

In the heat of the search, he must be capable of making diplomatic suggestions. Everyone he is communicating with is running on adrenalin; he must be calm. He is the one who must see the forest for the trees. He is the one who must tell an ambulance it is taking too long to get to the unconscious child and he is dispatching a second rig and sending them on a different route.

A good dispatcher feels responsibility for those he speaks to and for. He's a bit of a mother hen. Although he sits and works alone, his job is an exciting one, even if vicariously. Rescuers tend to develop respect for a good telecommunicator and will, once the crisis has been handled, radio to dispatch, "Good job. Thanks for your help." Over the radio, where emotions are kept under cover, this indeed is high praise.

The availability of an excellent dispatcher is important to a rescue; a bad one becomes detrimental as the scene falls apart, rescuers are working at cross purposes and needed gear is absent from the scene.

Dispatchers must have the ability to stay alert while sitting around for long periods of time. The sleeping dispatcher in your story who is awakening during the first fifteen seconds of his sixty-second window to dispatch emergency personnel could make a difference on victim outcome.

Job Description

Dispatchers tend to work eight-, twelve- or twenty-four-hour shifts. Most common nationwide are eight- or twelve-hour shifts. Some rural areas might schedule dispatchers to be on for thirty-six hours, then off for thirty-six. In these less-busy venues, a bunk and a TV might be provided for the on-duty dispatcher. Dispatchers working in noncosmopolitan areas might typically eat at their console and run to the bathroom between calls.

They tend to wear the uniform of the emergency team they dispatch for. Fire dispatch, for example, will wear a shirt with fire department patches and, frequently, an American flag. EMS dispatchers might wear the ambulance service's or rescue squad's insignias on the shirts of their uniform. If it is multidisciplined dispatch, they will have their own distinctive garments and patches.

Equipment

A dispatcher's tools are few. In addition to his own ability to think quickly, he has his computer console and a telephone headset. In big city dispatch centers where several calls are running at the same time, the room is frequently darkened, increasing focus upon the monitors' glow and quieting the space—the telecommunicators are not to be distracted. If it is an EMD center, they'll have medical protocol flip cards in front of them, or the flip cards might be loaded as software, flickering silently on-screen.

The most important tool a dispatcher has is radio waves. From the comfort of his chair, he can convey whatever information he wishes. At the other end, those in the field can let him know how they are progressing and what they need. In small towns where rescue personnel are on call rather than on duty, dispatch will use a tone to alert responders. This tone is the noise of a distinctive radio frequency. Each rescue group in a community—fire, police, EMS, extrication—might have a different-sounding tone that opens up their radios or pagers so they hear the call, even if they have not been scanning the frequencies. This system saves the dispatcher from having to make thirty different phone calls to alert rescuers, and it allows him to call out only the help that is needed. From the responders' point of view, being toned out enables them to react within their scope of training without being startled into attention for other teams' call outs.

Sometimes the dispatcher's radio will give him more than he wants. Depending upon atmospheric conditions, radio equipment with a twenty-mile range might pick up traffic from a thousand miles away. This is because dispatch radio frequencies, like commercial radio station frequencies, are reused throughout the U.S. A New Orleans dispatch center could be transmitting over the identical frequency as ones in Rapid City, Seattle and Hartford. The odd thing is that they will hear one another now and then. This phenomenon, known in the business as *skip* (as in, "I'm picking up skip tonight"), occurs when radio waves bounce up and down unpredictably between impenetrable atmosheric conditions and the earth's surface. Sometimes it is interesting to listen to skip because it is like a window that has suddenly been opened into another world. Tantalizing bits and pieces of rescue conversations float in and out. "Rescue 31, report to 16 Washington Street where a twenty-two-year-old female is. . . ."

Language

Dispatchers utilize what are called 10-codes. It is a clear shorthand that is easy for the responder to understand yet disguises what is going on from the eavesdropper with a home scanner. There is no universally accepted 10-code listing. One county sheriff's office might call a motor vehicle crash (or MVC as pros refer to it) as a 10-55 while the state police might refer to it as a 10-15. (Interestingly, rescuers used to refer to a vehicular impact as an MVA or motor vehicle accident. This is no longer politically correct since it conveys that the incident was not preventable.)

10-Codes: The Chatter of Rescue

Every town, city, county and state might have its own set of 10-codes. This listing gives you typical codes you can be comfortable borrowing.

10-1	can't copy (understand)
10-2	receiving well
10-3	go ahead (your turn to talk)
10-4	okay
10-5	relay a message
10-6	I'm busy; stand by
10-7	out of service/can't contact
10-8	in service
10-9	repeat
10-10	out of service but available
10-11	dispatching too rapidly
10-12	stay where you are
10-13	weather/road report

10-14	escort
10-15	have victim in vehicle
10-17	meet complainant
10-18	complete assignment ASAP
10-19	return to
10-20	your location
10-21	call by telephone
10-23	stand by
10-30	illegal use of radio
10-32	person with weapon
10-33	general broadcast/alert
10-34	mental subject
10-35	medical examiner needed
10-48	unattended death
10-55	MVC (motor vehicle crash)
10-60	lost hunter
10-61	hunting accident
10-62	drowning accident
10-66	snowmobile accident
10-79	plane crash
Signal 1000	keep all air travel to an absolute minimum; emergency situation in progress

If a SAR team found a snowmobile accident and a possible drowning on a lake in Idaho, the traffic might go like this:

"SAR 3; dispatch."
"Dispatch; SAR 3. 10-3?"
"Our 10-20 is Spectacle Lake. We've got a 10-66 with a possible 10-62."
"10-9, SAR 3. You're very 10-1."
"Our 10-20 is Spectacle Lake. We've got a 10-66 with a possible 10-62. Are you 10-2?"
"10-4, SAR 3. Be advised the 10-13 is deteriorating. Plan to 10-19 by 1600 hours. 10-3?"
"10-4. SAR 3 out."
"Dispatch out. KNGQ545 clear."

Ten-code talk can quickly become overkill in writings. Even some big city services are eliminating it in favor of normal conversation. But most of the country does continue to rely upon 10-codes. Don't overdo as in the example above. Just a sprinkling will add a touch of realism and authenticity to your writing.

There is also locale-specific radio jargon. PI refers to personal injuries, as in "There are multiple PI"; several people suffered PIs. In Vermont, Connecticut, Maine and Massachusetts, the dispatcher might direct the medic, "Give me a New England." He's asking the medical professional to call him on a land-line, or telephone, in this way because the region's old phone carrier (before NYNEX) was New England Telephone. "Call your A-unit" means your spouse just asked the dispatcher to have you phone home. If you're going home at the end of a long day, the dispatcher will get that message when you say you are going code-100.

Sometimes dispatchers use abbreviations. "What's your-20?" leaves out the 10 of 10-20. When dispatch asks that question, you know he is wondering where you are.

A typical conversation between a dispatcher and a SAR team leader would have the dispatcher indicate who he is, then ask for the leader, who would have a designated number such as 22. "Lincoln County Dispatch; SAR 22," the dispatcher might say. Or he might state who he is calling first, then identify himself: "SAR 22: Lincoln County Dispatch." One person speaks at a time since everyone is using a two-way radio. Sound can only travel one way at a time. This is why it is necessary to say something along the lines of "10-3?" when you are finished talking. There needs to be some mechanism to convey: I'm through talking. It's your turn now.

When a conversation has ended, both parties must say so. Some dispatchers like to use the word "Out" to indicate this. Others might terminate an exchange by reciting the frequency call-letters: "KNGQ545 clear."

When two rescue professionals depress the talk button on their radios at the same time, so that one of the speaker's words are blocked by the other's (which shouldn't happen if everyone waits for the signal that one person is finished talking), this is called *stepping*. The dispatcher would then inform the blocked voice, "You got stepped on. Repeat please."

Dangers

Sometimes it feels as if half the country is listening in on emergency frequencies. Dispatchers refer to all of those pairs of ears as *Scanner-land*. If you want to write authentic radio traffic, buy yourself a scanner at an electronics store and listen in yourself. At first the talk will be difficult to understand, but within a week, you'll understand what is going on. It's fascinating.

However, it's discomforting for the dispatcher who is on stage all the time. If he does not perform his job appropriately, the citizenry will know it.

The sorts of problems that may be transmitted to the public include inappropriate prioritizing of calls. To avoid the horrors we've all heard about when the 911 line gets jammed with nonemergency calls, some parts of the country have set up a 311 number to deal with incidents such as cats in trees or lost keys. Of course, these calls must also be triaged by a dispatcher. In either case, it is the dispatcher who must decide what is most important and what caller can wait for a response. It's a thankless task.

On the other hand, the dispatcher who is never sure what is life-and-death will overrespond, costing his municipality dollars as trucks roll and, in rural areas, as rescuers are toned out needlessly.

More and more frequently, dispatchers are finding themselves in court. They end up trying to explain why they did not dispatch a second responder when the first got lost, or how they decided a second caller with shortness of breath, which turned out to be a muscle pull, was more important than an elderly person who wandered from a nursing home and was found frozen the next day. Of all the rescue professionals, the dispatcher seems to be the one most recognizable; therefore, he is most exposed to liability complaints and most regularly singing the 911 Litigation Blues. Nameless and faceless, dispatchers are a lightening rod for frustration. It can happen to any telecommunicator who fails to do the job right the first time. Accordingly, as with all emergency rescue professionals, the move now is to slow down dispatch so mistakes are not made.

CHAPTER TWO

Searcher

If you are looking for a needle in a haystack, there are strategies ranging from scattering the hay willy-nilly up in the air to straw-by-straw moving it aside. A third choice might be to think about where last you saw the needle. Then take educated guesses about where it might be now, evolving a careful, reasoned strategy.

The distinction between these needle-searching methods is what differentiates professional searchers from enthusiastic and untrained participants. Search is one area of rescue where pros are scarce and bystanders, Boy Scouts and untrained firefighters are numerous and stand ready to work. So the searcher is not a common profession but is, instead, a role played by a mix of law enforcement, fire, EMS responders (if they are available) and the public—all untrained in search, but all anxious to help.

The access phase of a SAR operation might be handled by professional rescuers. Typically, this first component in the LAST process—*Locating*—is organized and led by professionals who are used to commanding, but are untrained in the management of search. The consequences of these fire and police chiefs' and sheriffs' actions and inactions are regularly disastrous. However, the public is unaware of the difficulties caused by uninformed leaders because the media doesn't know how it should work either. The public hears about the search that ended up as a body recovery, but does not realize that human error might have played a role; that the subject's life might have been saved if, for example, dog handlers and then a professional SAR team had been activated.

So this chapter focuses upon a reality that there are professionals who run countless small searches—the small-town cop, the suburban fire chief—but are not trained to do so! When they are successful, it is because the subjects are nearby, not hard to find. But their operations are not state of the art.

Given the rarity of a full-blown search, most fulfill the definition for a mass casualty incident because the professional management needs of the search exceed the talent available. (An MCI is defined as an event that overwhelms available rescue personnel and/or equipment.) Given the environment and time factors, a search can go downhill rapidly. Well-meaning managers who are unaware of how their techniques, such as they are, can obliterate clues and compound difficulties pale against the professional rescue manager, discussed in later chapters.

History of the Profession

The history of unorganized searches is the history of villages and neighborhoods in small villages. When a youngster wandered off from the hut or an elder failed to return from a trip to market, family members would get concerned and start looking. If their search was not successful after checking obvious places, they would find help in the form of manpower and leaders experienced in organizing people. Searching was successful because the area was small and familiar and the habits of the lost person were well-known.

When success was not immediately forthcoming, there was not much else to do. Families could wait patiently for the missing member to return. They could appeal to the supernatural or ascribe the disappearance to unexplained forces of evil. There were few options.

In most areas of this country, this is still the pattern for handling searches, and in most instances, the lost person is found quickly and easily. In fact, the subject usually shows up or finds the searchers because she was not lost but was off on a changed schedule or itinerary.

Problems arise in this otherwise successful search strategy as people venture further afield into less familiar territory. The adventurous journey into more challenging terrain and environments where they are likely to get into trouble and will be difficult to find. Searchers now look for strangers, for people whose behaviors are unknown to either the search organizers or the foot soldiers of search.

Education and Certification

At the local level, a few of those responsible for a small search—a police lieutenant or deputy sheriff—will have taken a "Managing the Search Function" course offered by the National Association for Search and Rescue (NASAR). This course, based upon the ICS, carries a prospective leader through the phases of a search:

- lost person questionnaire
- subject behavior
- characteristics of lost persons
- sequence for search planning
- probability of detection
- evaluating search urgency
- incident action plan
- situation status
- resource status
- rescue and recovery
- confinement methods
- investigation
- establishing the search area
- probability zones
- allocating SAR resources

Trained search leaders will understand how to go about the search, how to assign personnel in the field and how to spot and preserve important evidence.

At the local level, where searchers are not trained and the leader is a law enforcement professional only minimally knowledgeable about SAR techniques, methods may be logical but not state of the art. The real skill of these search leaders is that they are used to organization and command, and they have at their disposal people power to beat the bushes. Challenged to find a lost individual, they will check likely spots, then throw as many people as possible into what they guess is the search area . . . and keep their fingers crossed.

Qualifications

At this level of search, there are no qualifications for either a search manager or a searcher. The responsibilities rest with those who jurisdictionally have responsibility for the public safety under state or local statute.

These law enforcement or fire professionals do what makes sense to them. Firefighters are alerted, citizens come forth and a loose organization takes place for a line search. Hopefully, the person in charge is aware that once searchers tramp the search area, they disturb the scene sufficiently that search dogs become useless.

Law enforcement agents get involved quickly because there is always the chance that the missing person might be a victim or the search area might turn out to be a crime scene. So in addition to a fire chief who might be overseeing the search, a second jurisdictional figure might step in. From a writer's point of view, this has turf-war potential, particularly when the media gets wind of the activities. Sometimes the first person on-scene takes charge and keeps charge. There have been times when more than one professional responder conducts the search, or searches, sometimes side by side.

This phase of emergency rescue—so important since clues get obscured if it is not handled properly—has the most potential for disaster. Professionals not trained in SAR will not please later-appearing responders as the search widens and lengthens. Thankfully, civilian searchers are not used in unusual, dangerous circumstances. Winter rescue in severe conditions, avalanche rescue teams, urban SAR within collapsed buildings and searches conducted in rough terrain are undertaken by professionals.

Job Description

A professional law enforcement official finding herself heading a search will have to drop everything else and focus upon this event. A piece of the management has to do with dealing with the media, always hungry for lost-person stories.

The press, TV and radio combined with citizens wishing to get involved will cause the greatest headaches. Professional firefighters, usually drafted for searches, follow orders; they are unique in this aspect. Citizens are anxious to get in on the chance to be a hero, but are devastated when they find they are involved in a dead body recovery. Part-time, call firefighters also seem to delight in the

Predicting Lost Person Behavior

NASAR and other academic and research-oriented groups have collected and collated search statistics for hundreds of incidents. They have looked at lost person characteristics, trying to predict the likelihood of a particular lost person ending up in a particular area. It's like dropping different-sized needles into a haystack and measuring where each ends up so that the next time the same needle is dropped, you are better informed about where to start looking.

Prediction of "lost subject behavior" is based upon:

- category
- terrain
- weather
- personality
- physical condition
- medical history

Children act differently than adults when lost; teenagers and the elderly have specific characteristics when they become victims too.

The lay of the land will affect distance and direction. Escape routes, natural barriers, hills and drainage patterns need to be considered.

Weather can restrict the victim's movements. High or low temperatures, wind and humidity levels cause heat- and cold-related medical crises. The time the victim spends out in weather is also a determinate.

An assertive individual will act differently when lost than a subdued personality. Aggressive types tend to be survivors.

Your character with a broken leg will not be traveling very far. An individual used to jogging ten miles a day will be able to travel farther. Interestingly, the jogger is going to have a smaller chance of being rescued.

If the victim is suffering from any malady that might cause her to act strangely, her behavior while lost will be affected. It could also determine how far she will travel.

chance to be a searcher. But enough of the others who volunteer to help tend to lose focus once they are out of range and they go off half-cocked, creating headaches for the leader of the search. And no one is terribly good at following instructions.

We remember a search where volunteer firefighters, prior to being briefed (in fact, even before the chief was on-scene), went racing up a mountain in full turnout gear, missing a turnoff. They became the subjects of a second search when they became stranded on a talus slope a mile away from the search area without a radio or water. They were rescued long after the original subject had been brought down by his fellow climbers.

In situations like this, the pro leading the search becomes a nurse-maid, spending as much time dealing with amateur searchers who are improperly dressed—they suffer from heat-challenge in the summer and cold-challenge in the fall and winter—as they do with the originally missing subject.

The head of the search must deal with the subject's family, too. It is difficult for loved ones to understand why all of the forces seen in fictionalized TV tales and read about in books are not mobilized for their child or elderly mother. Searches do not start out with hundreds of searchers, ambulances standing by, dog teams, helicopters and National Guard troops. Searches expand organically; the key is to control that growth and link it with constantly changing circumstances and a developing sense of urgency as time passes. It is just as bad to have too many resources as it is to have too few. The media tends to present the most exciting search scenarios, which are fully involved.

The job description, then, for the untrained, small-town search manager is one of constant headaches, endless confusions and great difficulty.

Volunteer searchers have to show up and be willing to spend several hours beating the bushes looking for someone. It helps if they can follow orders and know their way around the woods, but neither characteristic is essential.

The odds are they will be expected to conduct a line search, a technique universally understood. Once on-site, they will form a straight line with as many other volunteers as available. If possible, one end of this line will be along a natural (stream) or man-made (road or trail) feature, while the other end will be marked with flags. Each searcher will be stationed close enough to the next that between them they can see all the intervening territory at all times. All are looking for clues as small as a gum wrapper or as large as a person.

On command, the line advances slowly through the search area. If someone finds a clue or wants to explore an area, she shouts or whistles, causing the leader to stop the line while the detailed search ensues. Finding nothing, a second command starts the line moving again. Found clues are not touched. Their location is tagged with fluorescent orange or pink plastic surveyors' tape. The item is left for the manager to evaluate. Progress is slow and careful.

A line search carefully conducted leads to a good chance of finding and reporting to base any clues found in a given area. But even moments of inattention or carelessness on the part of a single searcher can destroy the probability of detection for the entire search. That is why experienced, knowledgeable searchers such as rangers or SAR team leaders are in demand.

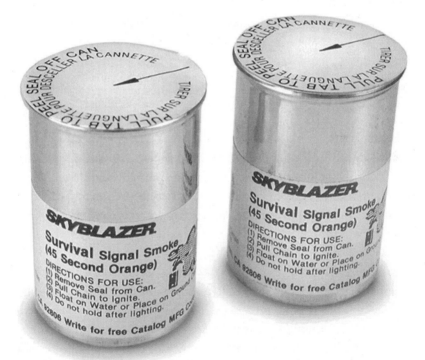

Skyblazer smoke cans can be used by searchers to signal others on the team. The cans, which can be placed on the ground or floated on water, produce intense, colored smoke visible for miles. (Photo © CMC Rescue, Inc., used by permission.)

Skyblazer signal mirrors are another means by which searchers can attract attention. The flashes are visible up to ten miles. Besides signalling, the mirror is also used for light control when tracking. (Photo © CMC Rescue, Inc., used by permission.)

Tools

Radio communication is essential during a search. Professional managers will distribute two-way radios to groups of searchers. Maps, usually copies of the relevant area of a topographic map, are indispensable. So are compasses. It's important for all search participants to know where they are, how to get to assigned territories and how to get back to base.

In addition to these rudimentary tools, searchers will need to be appropriately outfitted for the weather and the terrain. Decent, broken-in hiking boots are *de rigeur*. Some professional search managers evaluate their personnel by looking only at their feet. The type and condition of footwear is an indicator of how well somebody will do in the woods. No sandals and no sneakers.

All searchers going into the woods must carry a minimum of survival gear. Food, water, a flashlight for signaling, matches and additional clothing—all may become necessary if the searcher gets separated from the rest of the crew and has to spend a night in the woods. Yet this basic survival gear can be overlooked in the press of the moment. The consequences of ill-prepared searchers are overwhelming, making it likely that searchers will become lost, sick or injured, and the subject not found.

Language

As mentioned earlier, the word "subject" describes the focus of a search or rescue operation—the lost person. Once found, if the subject has been traumatized physically or emotionally by his ordeal and needs medical help, then he becomes a patient in need of rescue or evacuation. If the subject is found dead, a 10-48, then the search converts to a body recovery. Along the way, evidence about the subject is considered a clue to his whereabouts. The found subject is the biggest clue of all.

One of the big problems with untrained searchers is language. If they are using a radio, they tend to talk too much. Or the squawk and chatter of the radio causes stage fright and they freeze instead of depressing the button and communicating. This causes all sorts of problems, including the misunderstanding that a silent searcher might be lost or hurt as well.

Dangers

Take about a hundred people in various physical conditions wearing sneakers and inappropriate clothing and you'll find that the biggest danger is from within. Professional search team leaders will not allow an individual into the field who is not wearing the correct clothing for the weather and is not carrying twenty-four-hours worth of supplies in a backpack. This store of food, drink and clothing does double duty if a hungry, cold victim is found.

One of the obvious dangers is weather. Hypothermia, a life-threatening response to cold, is most common in the spring and fall in northern climates. In the dead of winter in northern Wisconsin, everyone knows not to go wandering outside without polar gear. But on a warm, sunny, spring-like day, people don't consider that the temperature will be dropping at sunset. Then they get lost with no sleeping bag and with the temperature dropping into the 40s. It's a killer and the kind of situation the professional searcher dreads and the amateur doesn't consider. A lost individual in the desert might be exposed to hyperthermia during the day, and hypothermia during the night. Both cold- and heat-related emergencies are compounded by dehydration. (See dehydration in the Appendix: Rescue Maladies.)

CHAPTER THREE

Dog Handler

Dogs are the most competent and cost-effective ground searchers. Whether it is a steaming summer day or a frigid winter storm, in desert or woodland, they produce. It is said that a search dog unit, one dog and one handler, can take the place of thirty line searchers. If there is an MCI or if visibility is poor, the ratio increases. And the more a team is used, the more efficient it becomes.

In literature, search dogs and handlers tend to be depicted working with other searchers in the same area. Or worse, they are called in after the human searchers. Neither should happen. This is often the case in the real world too. Unfortunately, after dozens of human scents have been added to the one of the subject, it is going to be difficult or impossible for the dog and handler to sort out the scene.

But when untrained fire or law enforcement officials are overseeing the search, dogs tend to be thought of as a last resort rather than the first team. If a search works correctly, it's because the dogs were in there early.

A search dog handler can be a professional law enforcement person who is on a canine patrol where both dog and handler are trained in search techniques as well as crime detection and criminal detention. Some prison systems or state police will have bloodhound teams trained to track escaped inmates. These law enforcement teams are available when there is a noncriminal search for a lost person. The more practice the dogs and handlers have, the better. In addition, there are individuals interested in dogs and in SAR who have taken courses and trained themselves and their dogs as a unit, available to respond when a subject needs to be found. The law enforcement professional teams receive compensation; it is becoming more common for the SAR units to receive per diem pay as well to at least cover expenses.

Both are pros.

History of the Profession

The relationship between dogs and early man may have come about because of the dog's sensory capacities. Dogs, who were tools long before they were pets, warned of unseen attack, protected and herded domestic animals and assisted in the hunt. All of these roles enhanced the pleasure of easy companionship humans found in canines. Still today, the dog handler will pay attention to her dog as it sees, sniffs and uncovers more than the handler can see or smell alone.

Dogs may have recognized the advantages of teaming up with humans too. SAR history shows that dogs have used their noses since the late tenth century to save lives. This followed the dog's natural instinct to hunt, and its desire to bond with and protect its human family.

The first police forces to formally use K-9 corps for criminal work were South Orange, New Jersey, and New York City. Both organized programs in 1907 and promptly reported that crime dropped more than 50 percent. Anyone who has ever experienced a dog bite (acutely painful) might believe the criminals decided to stay home rather than take the chance of being hunted by an excited German shepherd. It was reported in a 1911 news article that the dogs were taught that uniformed individuals were their friends and nonuniformed people were the enemy.

Other cities and even Canada's Mounted Police followed New York City's and South Orange's lead. Training programs began in earnest. Both the handler and the dog learned how to best search, whether for a robber or rescuing a lost person. Glen Ridge, New Jersey, formed a unit in 1910; Detroit in 1917; Berkeley in 1930; and, in 1944, the Connecticut State Police followed suit. Of all of these, the Royal Canadian Mounted Police K-9 section, formed in 1937, has the only still-active search dog program.

The modern era of police service dogs began about ten years later, in the 1950s. Baltimore's program became a prototype for others to follow where a dog lives with its handler and is integrated into the family unit. These home-based dogs are used in a variety of anticrime situations, and they have always been available for SAR. Today, every state has K-9 corps available whenever a lost person needs finding.

As people discovered the usefulness of police dogs for SAR, they set out to train them for private use. Informal search teams formed in areas where people frequently got lost. The American Rescue Dog Association (ARDA) organized in 1967 in response to this movement of volunteer groups. The California-based WOOF Search Dog Unit, a member of ARDA, has been the best known group during the past fifteen years. The group is comprised of about twenty-five teams, and its members are involved with over one hundred searches each year.

While its area is west of the Rockies, every area in the United States has access to search units who will travel long distances to assist in searches, usually with no remuneration or even gas reimbursement.

In the past, handlers placed emphasis on training specialized dogs by using different scenting concepts such as narcotics, rescue tracking and police or bomb detection. But today, handlers and trainers realize that, given the small trained-dog community, specialization is too restricting. When a handler is working with a search dog and finds that the lost child has been kidnapped, it would not make sense to suddenly call in a police dog. Today's handlers concede there really isn't a difference between a searching police dog and a search dog trained for SAR work.

Whatever the type, dogs and their handlers can perform a variety of functions. Handler and author Sandy Bryson says dogs can be trained to look for:
- people walking around, lying motionless, buried or hiding in debris or stuck in elevated positions
- things bearing human scent
- specific people or things identified to the dog by a scent article
- isolated scent from oils, gases, explosives, drugs and so on

It's thought that certain breeds might train more easily for these tasks, and those breeds have evolved as the choice of dog handlers.

However, there is the occasional handler who believes a strange breed or particular mix is best. What is sought is a medium-sized working breed with strength, stamina and agility. Ground searching dogs can be expected to cover an area as large as fifty miles in one day, then get up rested the next morning to repeat the process with the same amount of enthusiasm and energy. For SAR dogs who will be exposed to extremes of temperature, a double coat with stiff outer guard hairs and a softer undercoat will provide protection against both cold and heat.

Male dogs are larger and more muscular; females are more agile. The giant breeds are inappropriate, although Saint Bernards do have a reputation for avalanche work and Newfoundlands are adept at water rescue. Small breeds will find distances difficult. Short-legged dogs with large bodies have trouble with undergrowth and rubble piles.

For these reasons, golden retrievers, Labrador retrievers, Border collies and German shepherds are most frequently used. Bloodhounds, with their world-class noses, have a reputation as trackers but can be difficult to train and slow to learn. Their enthusiasm for *all* smells causes them to take off after everything, so it is an uphill battle to get them to stay focused.

You will not see a team of search dogs out in the field without encountering some crazy-looking mongrel with parts of all of the above-mentioned types, plus components of unexpected lineage. This dog might be the one outperforming his purebred peers. So what's the bottom line? Training of both the handler and dog and their working relationship are more important than bloodlines.

Education and Certification

The handler trains the dog and the dog trains the handler, and an experienced search dog trainer/handler should supervise that process. It is tough to train a SAR dog from a book. Never imagine that a dog and a handler with a book can retreat to the woods for a year and emerge as a successful SAR unit. The training itself and the actual SAR work require interaction with other people and dogs in a variety of contexts. Today, almost any community will offer a nearby SAR dog unit to train with.

This makes the whole concept a social affair, for the dogs as well as the handlers. It is also a labor of love. The more sophisticated SAR teams have required monthly weekend-long training sessions along with documented weekly private practice. This is work. It is not coincidental that the word "dogged" refers to persistence and stubbornness.

Search dog training, which is long and continuous, should begin within the first week of togetherness, as early as six weeks of age. As soon as the dog accepts the handler both as master and friend, canine education continues throughout the dog's lifetime. One trainer/handler refers to the three Rs of training: repeating the training so it seems to be an instinctive behavior; relating the training to the dog's intelligence so the handler expects only what the dog can deliver; and rewarding for appropriate behavior.

Throughout, the dog is being trained by the handler, and the handler is also being educated while learning about the dog. Both dog and handler have to be top-notch for them to function as a team. They must also be good at reading each other, understanding every gesture and nuance. Training is predicated upon pack behavior, status and reward, and the handler is the leader of the pack.

This leader needs to know what she is doing. Voice control is a piece of her training. She needs to understand how important tone as well as content is when she speaks to her hound. If the handler is anxious or confused, the dog will pick up on it through her tone of voice. Handlers are encouraged to tape their voice commands during practice to better know the hidden message being conveyed to their canine friends.

When the just-weaned, two-month-old pup begins its training, it is focused upon game-playing and socialization. But even the games can be search-oriented, such as "find the handler." Next, at six months, long, off-lead search exercises might begin. With age, the training becomes more complex with a variety of settings, times of day and types of weather; with other animals and all kinds of people; in the midst of commotion; and in and near cars, planes, choppers, ski lifts and boats. A well-trained dog takes anything and everything in stride. The dog must be willing to relieve itself on command, to bark or not bark when told. The dog cannot chase animals, including cats.

Handler Concerns

The handler has to keep on top of a list of many issues and responsibilities:

- Dog/handler readiness
- Workup procedures
- Commands and timing
- Dog's response to commands
- Dog's working temperament
- Strategy/flexibility/ability to revise
- Map reading/compass skills
- Portable radio skills
- Dog/handler endurance
- Dog/handler reaction to stress
- Responding to scent cone
- Relocating scent after wind shift
- Following scent to subject
- Tracking and trailing on command
- Recognizing fresh cross-track
- Staying with track (unless air scenting)
- Matching scent article or freshest scent
- Working to ignore interfering scent
- Dog's ability to do readable alert
- Handler recognizes readable alert
- Handler overrides or fails to direct
- Finds people or evidence
- Refind if appropriate
- Restart (alert/find on multiple subjects)
- Reward
- Obedience
- Agility
- Praise
- Emergency aid for dog and handler
- Transport
- Debriefing

With the growing frequency of the helicopter as a search tool, dogs and handlers need to be familiar with their operation and comfortable flying in them. They must also know how to rappel down from them. A rope dangling from the helicopter is belayed or anchored on the ground by a crew member. Dog and handler wear special harnesses that are clipped into a descending device. The dog rides between his handler's legs as they descend the rope. This is the drill when the chopper cannot land due to terrain. It allows search teams to be put down in areas that are inaccessible or would take hours or days to reach on foot. For similar reasons, a SAR team might also have to rappel down a cliff face.

In 1998, NASAR will work with the search dog community to establish training requirements leading to national certification. This development will standardize and quantify what a dog handler and dog need to know to be certified as competent for field work. NASAR publishes *SAR Dog Alert* several times each year, which is loaded with information about the dog SAR community's doings, including instruction, seminars and search reports.

Qualifications

Because of their close working relationship, a handler must love the dog, and the dog must feel close to and respect the handler. Once in a while, people will get involved with the SAR movement for glory or because they don't realize the time commitment. These people become impatient and harsh with their canines. As a result, these are the dogs that do not perform well. A basic ingredient of successful dog/handler work is that the dog has the sense that it is pleasing its handler. That is the one goal all dogs have and they need to get the message that they are succeeding. It is the handler's responsibility to love, praise, treat and reward the canine.

Just as a high-spirited dog is a necessity, so is an energetic handler. The dog will receive rewards, but the best canines find that the work is their reward. The eagerness of the handler plays an important part here. The handler's reward is like that of a proud parent.

Because the dog/handler relationship is crucial to the mechanics of a good search unit, it is important that when starting to train a new dog, a handler makes an accurate assessment of the dog's potential.

Regardless of pedigree and first impressions, some dogs will not adapt to the rigors of search training. The shrewd handler looks for early signs of eagerness for the task coupled with acceptance of a subservient role. A good nose for tracking and air-scenting work is a must, along with physical stamina. Openness and curiosity about other people and animals, including fellow search dogs, are integral. The dog must first be nimble and coordinated, then trained to take those natural qualities to the limit. SAR dogs have been agile enough to be taught to negotiate ladders with rounded rungs in collapsed buildings.

If a dog is judged wanting in any of these characteristics, no amount of training and attention will compensate. Handlers must be realistic and hardnosed early in their relationship with a new dog. They must cut their losses if they or others feel that the current dog won't work out, and the majority of dogs do not. The result is a dog responsive to its owner's commands and capable of making its own decisions when appropriate.

There is an old SAR dog story where a handler stretched while walking across a broad span bridge, and the dog, seeing the gesture for "Go!" went off the bridge. That trained dog could not reason for itself and didn't get another chance to.

Job Description

The job of the SAR dog unit involves a lifetime of training with constant day-to-day contact between the handler and the dog. Regular practice with other units—dogs and handlers—is required. The SAR dog unit's life is a refresher course. Whether a police team that gets involved in search or a SAR team unit, all must practice, practice, practice. They must also stay fit for the rigors of urban and wilderness search such as crawling through collapsed buildings or trekking through snow fields. Call outs can be infrequent—months apart and then three in a week. You never know what each search will entail and where it will take you.

The handler must be able to leave her regular work, drop everything at a moment's notice and be thrown into a stress-filled, chaotic, dangerous environment where nothing is sure or known. Both dog and handler must enjoy living on the edge, like the excitement of the chase and always be up for it.

Unless the SAR unit is affiliated with a policing entity, its work will usually be done with no compensation and little public understanding. The dog and handler must want to do it for its own sake.

The handler needs to be a competent medical first responder and should know CPR so she can take care of herself and whomever she finds. The handler must have practical knowledge of canine health and emergency care, must groom the dog daily and must never leave the search dog tied or kenneled, except in a commercial carrier.

From the nose-and-eyes point of view of a search dog at work, his job description is various. All search dogs are trained to work off a lead, meaning they are connected to their trainer by visual and auditory commands, not with a leash. They will sometimes range as far as a half-mile away from their handler, often leaving the handler scrambling to catch up.

Three Types of Canine Searches

There are three broad types of searches. The first type is a ranging search. If the search manager has little or no idea where the subject started from, then the dog is asked to cover an area, ranging back and forth along a handler-selected contour or compass heading, looking and sniffing for any clues. If it finds anything suspicious, the dog is trained to alert, which means to strike a particular pose that notifies the handler to come and check it out. The physical alert posture could be anything, ranging from the point of a hunting dog to a distinctive, excited circling. The cause of the alert may be a piece of evidence, a clue, the start of a scent trail or the object of the search. In any case, it is the handler's job to discern the cause of the alert and to decide the next step. By ranging back and forth along a line, the dog searches a given corridor of land. It is the handler's job to be certain this particular search corridor is the one assigned, or to be able to define the area on a map so that search command can know which areas have been searched and which areas still need to be covered. The width of the search corridor and the time it takes the dog to cover it are both determined by the nature of the terrain.

The classic example of this first kind of search is avalanche work. The search manager divides the terrain into sections, and search priorities are assigned to each section depending upon educated guesses about where the victim may have ended up. Based upon these probability-of-detection guesses, each dog/handler unit is assigned a section to search rapidly. When the dog alerts, the handler uses an avalanche probe, a long aluminum or fiberglass pole, to blindly feel for a body under the snow. If the alert is confirmed, then dog and handler dig like crazy to recover the hopefully still-alive victim.

Another specialized ranging search uses dogs to sniff for the final location of a possible drowning. Water currents, like air currents, move scents. As the smells reach the surface, dogs can pick them up. Divers are brought in after two dogs have independently alerted in the same area. Search dogs on water don't replace divers, but they do narrow the area that must be investigated.

The second type of dog searching has the dog and handler starting with a scent item, which tells the dog who or what he is looking for, and often with a point where the subject was last seen. Here the dog follows a scent cone or plume, a long triangle of dispersed scent that narrows and concentrates as the dog gets closer to the subject. If the scent is lost, then the dog has to range widely, trying to relocate it. If the scent trail has been crossed by the target, the dog is expected to recognize and follow the fresher, newer scent plume. This is air-scent work where searching dogs lope through the terrain, noses up and eyes active.

The third type of dog searching is tracking, which in the public eye is the province of the bloodhound although in practice any dog with a good nose is capable of tracking. Bloodhounds, because of the wonders of their noses, are the most common trackers. Here the dog is put onto the track where the target was or passed through. The dog is expected to determine the direction of travel based upon the freshness of the scent, and then to follow the trail to the target. If a bloodhound loses the scent, he is trained to range the area in progressively wider search patterns until the trail is found again.

A track, because it is composed of scent particles lying on the ground rather than a plume being wafted by the wind, is more durable. Tracking dogs can work later in the search than air-scenters. When bloodhounds are on track, they will be seen running along the trail, noses to the ground, tails wagging. They may start baying as, according to the scent trail, the search narrows.

Bloodhounds' big, floppy ears, loose folds of facial skin and free-flowing saliva all are part of the scent-tracking mechanism. The folds and ears work as a funnel to bring smells to the nose. Saliva traps scent particles. Dragging ears and jowls turn over dead leaves and twigs on the ground, releasing scents. In many ways, a working bloodhound is a vacuum, sucking up smells as it ruffles the surface. Long before science understood the uncanny abilities of a dog's nose, bloodhounds were so named because they were believed capable of following a trail of blood left by wounded prey.

At the conclusion of a search segment, the handler is expected to report to the search manager. What areas were searched? How rugged was it? What were the ground-surface conditions? How accurate are the maps distributed to all handlers? Based upon the terrain, what would the handler guess the probability of detection to be if the subject were in that piece of the wilderness? A good debriefing is imperative because a search is a never-ending shift of probabilities and guesses; accurate, concise information from one sector gives the manager reliable information on which to base the next set of assumptions.

Equipment

A good handler will carry into the field all of the equipment she and her dog might need. This includes the usual collar and lead along with a sling or harness to raise or lower both members of the team from a helicopter. The handler's backpack's contents need to include survival and first aid gear for a variety of environments, temperatures and conditions for both man and beast.

Both dog and handler dress in high-visibility outerwear, frequently fluorescent orange vests worn by dog and handler alike so they can be spotted by other search members and not misidentified by hunters. The team needs to carry twenty-four hours' worth of food and water as well as treats and toys, which the dog recognizes as rewards.

All this gear is packed and ready to go in advance of the call out. The handler will have to review the contents of her backpack on a regular basis, substituting out-of-season gear for new items. The handler must carry on her back all of the gear that she, the dog and the subject, when found, might utilize during a day and night in the field. This needs to include overnight necessities such as a sleeping bag and tent.

Language

The following list explains the most common terms used by dog handlers:

AIR-SCENTING CANINE Locates humans by following airborne scents to their source.

HANDLER Also called search specialist or trainer. The dog's trainer is responsible for directing the dog and helping it locate a subject.

RAFT A grouping of shed skin cells. A flake of dandruff is a large raft; an individual skin cell is a small raft.

REFIND Open area search procedure where a dog locates the subject, returns to his handler and leads the handler back to the subject.

SCENT The smell of the human body the dog follows. Body odor is a gas exuding an aroma from shed skin cells being digested by bacteria.

SCENT CONE Plume of smell increasingly widened and diluted by wind and other environmental conditions. One end of the scent cone is wide and is the minimal level a dog can detect; the other end is pointed at the scent source or target.

SECTOR The area assigned to a SAR unit defined by topographic or man-made features as they appear on a map. They can range from 40 to 200 acres depending upon the urgency of the search and the number of searchers.

SENSE OF SMELL Information collected by sensory cells located in the nostrils. Humans have 5 million such cells and dogs have 125 to 220 million.

Commands

The following orders are used by dog handlers when working with their dogs.

ASK! Training the dog to check with its handler before doing anything unusual or different.

COME! Immediately return to handler.

CRAWL! Enter a confined space such as a cave, cranny or small air space in a collapsed building.

DOWN! A variation of stay; lie down and remain there.

DROP IT! Release whatever the dog has in its mouth.

FREE DOG! The dog is off-lead; it is time to go to work.

GO BACK. Directional command.

GO OUT. Directional command, e.g., through a door.

GO THIS WAY. Directional command.

GO TO. Directional command, e.g., to a known spot.

HEEL! For a right-handed handler, the dog returns to the handler's left side with its shoulder at the handler's hip. For a working dog in the field, this is home base.

HUP! Jump!

HURRY UP! The dog is to quickly accomplish whatever it is doing, including relieving itself.

LEAVE IT! Move off a scent or visual observation.

MOVE! Get out of the way.

READY TO WORK OR WATCH HIM! Work up commands that build enthusiasm and get the dog pumped to work.

STAY! Whether sitting, standing or on the ground, the dog is not to move from that site, staying out of harm's way but ready to work. No matter where the handler is, the dog will stay, e.g., a dog in a car will be told to, "Stay."

STEADY! Be careful in a difficult situation requiring agility.

WAIT! Pause briefly; wait for the handler to catch up.

Dangers

Just as a SAR dog and handler save lives, they often find themselves in serious situations. Again, in rescue work, making oneself a second victim is considered bad form. The fact that a dog is doing the work of perhaps thirty rescuers makes the scene safer in terms of overall human costs, but it does not reduce the dangers to the search team. The better trained the dog is, the more likely it is that it will find itself in risk-filled situations. This dog is valuable because it is able to check out a hazardous site rather than a human.

Because of their proportion and coordination, dogs search unsafe scenes efficiently. This puts them in the most dangerous situations. The handler is responsible for overall scene safety and awareness of factors that can cause the environment to change such as deteriorating weather, snowpack conditions, fire or flooding. These are conditions the dog cannot be expected to know; the human must keep both of them out of danger.

The other side of the coin is when the dog finds itself with a problem that the handler knows nothing about. The handler might call, "Come!" and the dog appears, barreling out of the woods with a grizzly in pursuit!

CHAPTER FOUR

Ranger

Rangers' responsibilities are far-reaching. They can be county, state or federally affiliated. They are the law enforcement officials within the land where they have jurisdiction. In addition to catching poachers, responding to suicides and helping stranded tourists, they might provide EMS if they are certified and state licensed as medical providers.

The fine points of a ranger's work depend upon his assignment, physical skills and training. For example, a National Park Service ranger at Bunker Hill might converse with tourists. One in Mt. McKinley will be a winter rescue expert. The Grand Canyon ranger might be a SAR specialist.

The ranger's job is diverse and for particular rangers, SAR would only be a piece of it. There are places where people regularly get lost, such as in the Great Smoky Mountains National Park, and there the rangers' first responsibility would be SAR response. This diversity is true for national park rangers, and for rangers at the state level as well.

In less-populated states, rangers are the legal entity responsible whenever and wherever a person is reported overdue. Often sheriffs, fire chiefs and police chiefs will ignore the ranger's authority for as long as possible. However, at some point—often when amateurish attempts have failed, the scene has been contaminated and the search is spiraling out of control—rangers will be called in to create order out of chaos. Luckily, these broadly cross-trained individuals have the physical and mental resources to deal with

Rescue operations for rangers often involve dangerous terrain, such as this vertical evacuation. (Photo © CMC Rescue, Inc., used by permission.)

whatever they are encountered with.

Rangers used to be perceived in films and books as masculine, powerful, quiet, comfortable in the woods, at home with Mother Nature and by choice not in much contact with their fellow humans. Today, rangers are still overwhelmingly male. But females are entering the ranger's world in greater numbers and at all levels. These sometimes tiny, soft-spoken women have proven themselves as forces to be reckoned with.

It is overlooked that these men and women are first and foremost professional law enforcement officials. And secondly, they are guides and liaisons between the outdoors and the public. It is as police that they manage the search function.

History of the Profession

In the U.S., rangers' roots go back to the frontier. As the west was settled in the 1800s, rangers and U.S. Marshals were the law of the land. Rangers had the responsibility of covering the vast open spaces, bringing some measure of order to the Old West. The Texas Rangers are the best known example in this country. In Canada, the Royal Canadian Mounted Police are a rough equivalent.

Gradually, the open spaces narrowed. States were carved out of the annexed territories. Towns and counties were incorporated. Each new government agency created and ran its own police force to keep order. As the federal government began to set aside large parcels of land in the late 1800s and early 1900s, the national park system was created. Rangers were the logical choice to oversee those parcels often meant to be forever wild.

States followed suit with their own park systems and also chose to designate their park police as rangers. Today, in either a federal or state setting, rangers are a uniformed agency with full law and investigative powers in all areas of their jurisdiction. Several types of patrols are used to ensure visitor and park protection including foot, cruiser, horse-mounted, marine, motorcycle, motor scooter, helicopter and plainclothes. In addition, park rangers serve as hosts and information specialists to millions of annual visitors.

Education and Certification

Today's ranger is a college graduate with a variety of skills that allow him to enter this highly competitive and desirable field. Prior to acceptance, aptitude exams are administered. Along with didactic screening exams that include field biology and ecology, ranger candidates must pass a physical fitness test of vigor and endurance.

After acceptance, rangers are law enforcement trained and certified. Once in the service, depending upon their interests and employers' needs, they might receive training in specialities such as technical rescue, search, CPR, EMS, wilderness first responder (WOFER) and backcountry guiding. In terms of his job description, a ranger could be anything from a backcountry ranger/EMT in Texas' secluded Big Bend Park where he might see five hikers a week to a guard/tour guide at the Washington Monument addressing thousands of people daily.

The courses relating to search-leadership that the ranger will have taken might include "Planning Section Chief for Search and Rescue" and "Managing the Lost Person Incident" (formerly "Managing the Search Function"), both offered by NASAR.

Qualifications

Search is an emergency; some sort of response should happen immediately. What that means for a ranger involved in SAR is that he has to be authoritative, decisive and flexible as events require a change of plans.

He has passed aptitude and endurance tests and is in excellent physical shape, whether a veteran of the service or a brand-new college graduate. He is an avid outdoorsman, used to counting upon his own devices.

But this individual is also tourist-friendly, a social animal. At various points in his career, a ranger will be both on his own in the wilderness and in charge of hundreds of people organized on a search. His main credential is his ability to command, whether on a hasty search involving a few advance runners or a week-long line search involving a thousand volunteers. For these and other reasons, a ranger is well-educated, interested in a variety of topics, emotionally stable and flexible.

While this description of qualifications might appear larger than life, it is accurate.

Job Description

The ranger is trained to be the administrative head of a rescue operation, but he might act as a first responder when a hiker is reported hurt in a crevice. Or it is the ranger who will go out tracking, hoping to locate a lost victim and end a search operation before he has to initiate it. The ranger job description overlaps with that of other rescue specialists, except for a search operation. When a full-blown, well-organized search unfolds, a ranger should be running it. This is not always the case. There are situations when they take over naturally, and others when they should be called in but are not, or are called in late in the game.

When someone is reported overdue, the first step prior to a search is to organize a hasty team of two or three who, carrying only water, will move as fast as they can through the area with the most potential for locating the subject.

As the ranger expands the incident, he takes the lead role. He utilizes his training both in his NASAR courses and the ICS—a system used throughout the country to institute an organized response to a disaster—to organize a large-scale search. (See page 12 for the ICS flow chart.)

As the hasty team roams, professional SAR teams are placed on standby through phone calls or by pager. If the hasty team does not find the subject, search dog units, line searchers and helicopters are alerted.

Once forty-eight hours have passed, a full-action search is mobilized. Line searchers are staged nearby, ready to go into action if the dogs are unsuccessful. Choppers take off; SAR teams are elevated to call-out status.

The ranger who is incident commander gathers information about the subject, terrain and weather conditions. Family and friends are interviewed using a lost person questionnaire. This form, about a dozen pages long, will collect the following data:

- The plans the victim made for the cross-country ski weekend or two-hour summer hike, including the destination and estimated time of return.

- The type, color and size of clothing he was wearing, with detailed descriptions of each item from his sunglasses to the tread pattern on the sole of his boot. A scent article of his clothing will be requested in the event that search dogs are activated.

- Where was the victim last seen? Who saw the victim? How come? Who was the last person to have a lengthy conversation with the subject? What was he doing at that time? Which way did he leave? What was his mental attitude at that time? Was the victim unhappy or complaining of anything? Was an exhausted/hot/cold appearance noted?

- How outdoor savvy is the victim? Has he been in this area before, taken any courses in outdoor activities? What about medical training? What kind? Was the subject ever a scout or scout leader? What about overnight experience?

- Has the victim ever been lost before? What were the circumstances?

- How fast of a hiker is the victim? Would you expect him to follow trails? Any climbing experience? Other athletic experience?

- Is the victim a smoker? What brand? How often? What about drinking? How often and what brands? Does he use any drugs? How about candy or gum?

- Is the victim a leader or follower? What hobbies and interests does he have? What kind of personality traits does the victim exhibit?

- Is there any legal trouble? Personal difficulties? Is the victim divorced?

- Does the victim attend church? What faith? What are his values, philosophy? Any emotional problems? Is the victim the type to throw in the towel or keep trying?

- What is the victim's education?

- Who is the victim's closest friend and relative? Does he have a fictional hero?

- Is the victim healthy? What is his medical history? Who's his doctor? Is the victim physically challenged? On any medications?

What happens if the medications are not taken? What is his eyesight without glasses or contact lenses? Does the victim carry extra glasses or contacts?

• Describe all of the gear the victim has: backpack, tent, sleeping bag, ground cloth, climbing gear, water bottle, fire starter, compass, knife, skis, snowshoes, crampons, money, credit cards, food and map. How competent is the victim at outdoor activities?

If a group is overdue, the form asks about clashes within the group, intra-group dynamics and the leader's experience. If the lost person is a child, there is a different set of questions.

When the ranger has completed the missing person questionnaire, he will be prepared to make educated guesses about where in a limitless universe the lost person might end up. Based upon his data, the ranger must evaluate the level of urgency.

If the subject is young and alone, timing gets cranked up a notch. But if the subject is an experienced outdoorswoman who is overdue, the timing is less serious. The criticalness of the timing is determined by various factors. Terrain can be a factor, for example, if that trained female is in an area known for rock falls, the search will be more pressing. Provisions carried by the subject play a factor as does the weather. Based upon such considerations, decisions must be made: Is this a search where all of the stops ought to be pulled out? Where even line searching ought to continue all night because the person is unlikely to survive unless found in the next six hours?

To guide him in this and other decisions, the ranger as search manager will use a 3″ × 7″ inch orange, plastic-covered flipbook published by NASAR. It's bursting with statistics and probabilities on subject behavior based upon the actions of similarly profiled lost individuals. (Order the *Incident Commander Field Handbook: SAR* from the NASAR bookstore at [703] 222-6277.) An analogy would be the scattering of needles into a pile of hay. Ten percent will go straight into the pile; 70 percent will bounce, coming to a stop four inches from the landing spot; and the remaining 20 percent will skitter down the side of the pile and end up on the floor.

Some probabilities from NASAR's flipbook:

Typical sectoring of containment area

The following map would be used by the ranger to plan a search. Trails and natural boundaries are used whenever possible to define search segments. Each SAR team is assigned to a sector. Note the last known place (LKP) at the ⊗. Never forget that the entire area outside of the containment area is always a statistical, though improbable, possibility.

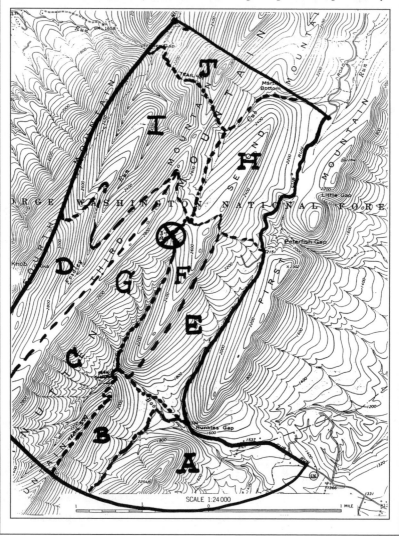

- Fifty percent of all overdue persons are poorly equipped and improperly clothed. About half will be found dead.
- One- to three-year-olds might not even realize they are lost. They wander in search of a comfortable place to lie down and sleep—such as inside a log, under brush or under a hanging rock. They are usually are found within a quarter mile of the point last seen (PLS).
- Older toddlers move more, are scared when they realize they are lost and will search for something familiar. Because they've been trained to stay away from strangers, they might hide from searchers. On average they are found less than a half mile from the PLS.
- Preteens have some directional skills. They are confused and unhappy in unfamiliar environments. They worry about being punished, like to gain attention and can be sulky, so they might not answer when called. As night falls, however, they are more interested in being found. They tend to follow water courses or climb up to look for familiar sites.
- The elderly act differently than young adults. They might be senile and their attention will be easily diverted. Childlike, they will exhaust themselves without realizing it. They often think in the past rather than the present. They may not hear search calls. The elderly average one-and-a-half miles movement down from the PLS.

The ranger now goes through the gathered information regarding probabilities and reaches conclusions not initially obvious. As mobilization of rescue resources begins—line searchers, helicopters, SAR teams, technical teams—confinement methods are decided upon.

The process of search is one of elimination, so it is imperative to limit expanses to be searched. The question the ranger must answer is: What is the perimeter of the area where the subject might have traveled to, given the time elapsed and the lost person profile?

Once that containment area has an invisible border drawn around it (and a real line on everyone's map), all traffic to and fro must be monitored. Roadblocks are set up and civilians are sent into the woods along the line; others are posted on high points. Spools of line are attached to workers' backpacks and they walk the woods,

---

Who's Lost?

For reasons that become obvious, the most aggravating search is known as the bastard search. Thirty-six hours into the search, a hasty team has failed to find the subject; the hovering choppers have landed twice and are deploying for the third time; the dogs are in the field and two-hundred professional personnel from surrounding SAR teams have arrived and are being fed into the mess.

At this point, a reporter from the local paper walks up and says to the search leader, "Sergeant Miller, my editor just called this lost guy's home to get background info, and he answered the phone. What gives?"

The no-longer lost person is embarrassed at getting turned around in the first place. And, even though he knew all of the stops had been pulled out to find him, when he came across a containment sign:

JOE: THIS WAY ↗

he just went home without notifying anyone he was safe.

The bastard search. It happens enough for everyone in SAR to experience it and watch for it.

---

leaving string in their wake. Dangling arrows pointing to the road or base camp are attached to the line.

As the perimeter is secured and nonsearch persons are escorted out, rescue professionals have gone 10-10; they report that they are on-scene.

Equipment

The ranger will wear militarylike uniforms with Smokey the Bear hats. In his briefcase, the ranger-in-charge (also referred to as the incident commander [IC] or search manager) will carry laminated maps of the confinement area, lost person questionnaires and a dozen other forms, tape, pads, pencils, overhead projector pens and transparencies, the orange NASAR *Incident Commander Field Handbook: SAR*, search software on diskettes and listings of rescue resources.

The vest and helmet of the ranger in charge of a large-scale rescue will have *Incident Commander* signage. Generally in such a search, signs and directional arrows will be posted as a way to organize the scene. We once responded as the medical component of a SAR operation hours into the wilds in our new convertible. We parked and went to check in and get some grub. Upon our return, we discovered a large, wooden sign saying "Medical Station" placed against our vehicle's windshield!

Language

The following list of terms and abbreviations are used during search-and-rescue operations.

CONFINEMENT Drawing a visual fence around the LP, and the surveillance of that line to be aware of the LP's crossing.

HASTY TEAM Immediate response in the form of physically fit, clue-conscious searchers who hustle through most likely area prior to the activation of the professional search teams.

IAP Incident action plan.

IC Incident commander.

LKP Last known place where a search area is defined. A circle is drawn as the subject could travel in any direction from the LKP.

LP Lost person.

PLS Point last seen.

POA Probability subject is within search area.

POD Probability of detection.

POS Probability of success

Note: $POA \times POD = POS$

RECOVERY Bringing someone out dead.

RESCUE Bringing someone out alive.

SITSAT Situation status.

Dangers

When involved in rescue work, ranger dangers are the usual faced by other rescuers. The terrain might be rough; the operation may be difficult. The one difference between the ranger and other professional rescuers is that the ranger is a law enforcement officer. He packs a gun. That distinction carries with it a plethora of other perilous possibilities.

Those Who Access

CHAPTER FIVE

Firefighter

When there is a structure fire with victims trapped inside, firefighters are trained to bring victims to safety, to a place where they can be taken care of by medical personnel. This second step in fire rescue—locating the victims and dragging or leading them to safety—provides access. While most rescue is focused on getting providers to the victims where they, in turn, can stabilize and treat, the environment of a working fire is so hellish that the rescuer needs to get the victims to help rather than the reverse.

Only the firefighter has the equipment, training and experience to enter a burning building and roam around, searching for trapped victims. Only the firefighter has trained for hours on end, donning full protective gear, crawling through smoke-filled practice towers with zero visibility, and locating and dragging to safety adult-sized, deadweight dummies.

A structure fire is not a place for the faint of heart. No one other than a professional, rescue-trained firefighter is allowed to enter a burning building no matter how many women and children are hanging out of the upper-story windows.

In the media, firefighters are portrayed rolling their ladder truck up to the inferno. Rescue is made by racing up the extended ladder, slinging victims over a brawny shoulder and carrying them back down to safety. This is the fire rescue that makes good newspaper and TV pictures. While this does happen, the bulk of firefighters' saves are made by room by room sweeps through buildings, looking for persons overcome by smoke. This less graphic picture is significantly more perilous to the participants, but is the way it tends to unfold.

Fire rescue is not for the faint of heart. Here, firefighters climb ladders toward a building engulfed in smoke. After entering the building, the firefighters will conduct room-by-room sweeps in search of victims overcome by smoke. (Photo used by permission of Harvey Eisner.)

Most urban fire departments have teams specifically trained for the perils of rescue. These personnel are routinely dispatched to all structure fires, whether the building is just beginning to show smoke or is fully involved. More commonly and in less populous areas, firefighters are cross-trained in a variety of firefighting activities, which include victim locating and accessing.

History of the Profession

Philadelphia's Ben Franklin established the first organized fire department. These early departments were subscribed to as a form of insurance. The company's name (which is why fire groups still are called companies) in the form of a cast-iron logo was emblazoned on the front of each insured building as proof that the structure in question was protected by a particular company. Some fire companies, like Atlantic Engine Company #2, still hold onto their old-timey names and traditions.

From the outset, the purpose of the fire department was three-fold: (1) extinguish the fire; (2) rescue whomever is inside; and (3) prevent the fire's spread to neighboring property. In modern times, the second of those three has been expanded into a variety of rescue activities. In addition to fire rescue, extrication from collapsed buildings and crushed vehicles, rope rescue from dangerous heights and depths, and hazmat response are the three most common fire department rescue activities. (See the appropriate chapters for discussion of these activities.)

Fire departments today are in a state of flux. Due to the advent of smoke detectors, enforced structure and building codes, sprinkler systems and fire department's proactive safety training, the incidence of fire has plummeted in the last twenty-five years. Firefighters have less and less firefighting work. Towns and cities find themselves with large fire payrolls, huge equipment budgets and diminishing demands. Many municipalities have expanded the firefighter's job description and have chosen to involve firefighters in safety programs which, if successful, increase their fire inactivity.

Traditional avenues of budget cutting, laying off personnel and centralizing facilities haven't worked because when there is a fire, a rapid response with sufficient crew from a nearby station is essential.

At the same time, lay-offs and reductions in equipment budgets have been difficult to realize because of active and sophisticated fire lobbies. Fire departments and fire unions such as the International Association of Firefighters are politically savvy and well-organized at both local and national levels. Firefighters have the proximity and time to continue to be well-organized. Firefighting is a team game; the impetus to join together in battle, whether political or fire-related is instilled within these men and women.

Recently, as budget cuts loom in response to fewer fires, firefighters have been actively attempting to control emergency medical services. Those who remember the television series *Emergency!* with Johnny and Roy know that fire departments frequently trained the first paramedics. Nationally, however, the firefighter response to the advent of EMS was, "We don't do that hand-holding stuff. We're *firefighters*." But as layoffs and pay reductions were realized, fire departments began to vie for the control of street medicine. Its federal lobby, the Congressional Fire Services Institute, is powerful. In many cities, fire departments have been successful at expanding their rescue bases, much to the chagrin of EMS providers who say, "We're medical providers. Don't ask us to deal with *fires*."

However, this is not true everywhere. In many communities, fire services are being thwarted in their attempts to control EMS, as parallel municipal or private EMS services have become well-entrenched and because there is no direct correlation between providing street medicine and fighting fires. According to an old EMS joke, fire services want paramedics as part of the department so the medics can regularly turn over idle firefighters, keeping bed sores from developing.

An interesting new development is the privatization of fire services. Just as proprietary ambulance services have contracts with towns, corporations are now offering communities complete firefighting packages including equipment, personnel, benefits, payroll and training. And towns and cities are buying in on them.

Education and Certification

Firefighters who enter burning buildings might well be cross-trained, educated at a firefighting academy and also trained and certified as, for example, an EMS-providing emergency medical technician (EMT). This is helpful when an injured victim is located and must be moved. Usually though, the firefighter's rescue job is to find and bring out fire survivors or victims. To accomplish this, they need to be trained in three specific skills: the use of self-contained breathing apparatus, techniques for searching in fire, and various drags and carries.

Self-contained breathing apparatus (SCBA) education and certification are required for all firefighters before they enter a burning or smoke-filled structure. This gear is analogous to divers' self-contained underwater breathing apparatus (SCUBA) developed and popularized by Jacques Cousteau. But SCBA is not appropriate for underwater use. The point of SCBA is that it allows a firefighter to breathe and work in a noxious environment because it supplies fresh, smokeless air through a combination of an air tank, rubber hose and face mask. Most fatalities in a fire are caused by smoke laden with toxic fumes—the gasses produced by the combustion of modern upholstery are deadly—rather than by the fire itself.

Prior to the invention of SCBA, firemen used their beards to purify the air they were breathing when in a smoky environment. They would dip their heads in a bucket of water, then pop their beards into their mouths as a smoke filter. This is why so many old fire company photos show firemen bearded beyond contemporary standards. Interestingly, SCBA usage has forced fire companies to prohibit beards because they do not allow a perfect, airtight fit of the SCBA mask.

SCBA training includes familiarity with the equipment, the actions taken to don the gear and how to function while using it to breathe. Personal safety and time are the issues. Malfunctioning SCBA shortens the time a firefighter can be in an involved building; broken SCBA can kill the wearer. So personnel are taught how to check their apparatus, making sure there is sufficient air pressure and that the various flow and warning devices are working. Then the face mask needs to be seated so the pure air the firefighter needs to breathe is not leaking out. Conversely, the mask seal must be tight to keep carbon monoxide and other gases from entering the firefighter's respiratory system.

Wearers must get used to the equipment, which is like carrying twelve bricks on ones' back. One tank or bottle of air (not oxygen) will provide about fifteen minutes of working time. Even though all of this gear causes claustrophobia, the wearer can't be nervous while wearing it. Jitters coupled with the physical exertion of searching a burning building cause rapid breathing or hyperventilation, and the full fifteen-minute air supply will be reduced by as much as half.

To become SCBA-certified, firefighters must complete a timed checking-and-donning test and then, while blindfolded, negotiate an obstacle course. While wearing the clumsy firefighter's turnout gear—pants, coat and boots—the probationary firefighter walks to the truck with its hanging SCBA units attached to the side. The challenge is to check out and put on the SCBA while an examiner observes, stopwatch in hand. Then, while wearing the gear, a hood is placed over the applicant's head. In a pitch-black, smoke-filled tower, the student feels his way through a series of barriers, obstructions and impediments while accomplishing set tasks.

During this test and totally at random, the tester will simulate a snagged air hose, which becomes disconnected from the mask or tank. Faced with a sudden loss of air, the firefighter must stay calm, reconnect the hose while holding her breath and, using only her sense of touch through heavy gloves, go on about her rescue business. The point is to ensure that all SCBA activities become second nature. In a burning building, it is too late to wonder what hose connects to what valve.

Training in SAR inside a burning building focuses on efficient movement with zero visibility. The idea is to effectively sweep through the structure to find humans and, at the same time, preserve a way out. Firefighters always sweep in teams, using the buddy system.

Firefighters are taught a variety of lifts, drags and carries to bring victims out of danger. As part of the training, heavy, lifelike mannequins are hidden in the practice building awaiting rescue. Since 1992, there have been world championship competitions, called the Firefighter Combat Challenge. One of a number of timed tasks is dragging a 175-pound dummy around.

The International Association of Firefighters and the International Association of Fire Chiefs have put together a complete program, titled

Firefighters are taught a variety of methods for bringing victims to safety. Here a parent does the heavy lifting, carrying a child down a ladder. The firefighter coaches the rescuer through the process. (Photo used by permission of Harvey Eisner.)

IAFF/IAFC Fire Service Joint Labor Management Fire Service Wellness/Fitness Institute. Fire services will be urged to follow its criteria, but hopefully will not be expected to remember its name!

Qualifications

Firefighters must be physically capable of doing the work. Their gear is heavy and cumbersome; the protective clothing they wear is hot and bulky. Their working environment is not conducive to life. It is confusing and confining with poor visibility. Firefighters must be able to keep their cool under scary conditions.

There are no specific requirements for a rescuing firefighter outside of the regular firefighting criteria. The tradition is that personnel on the first arriving truck conduct the building search while those coming on-scene after them attack the fire. This means that at one fire, a man may search a building and at the next, he might be responsible for hydrant connections. A big city fire department might work somewhat differently with specialized fire rescue teams.

Job Description

Firefighters as rescuers are expected to be competent in systematic room-by-room exploration. The decision might be made that one partner goes down the left side of a room while the other half of the team searches the right wall's floor area. Or two buddies might stretch out a ten-foot tether between them; while one crawls along a wall, the other remains in the center of the room. The rope will alert them to objects or people in the room. Hose lines can be held onto as a marker for the return trip.

Sometimes firefighters can't get out the way they entered. They must then find an exterior door or window and be capable of lowering themselves down.

When a rescue team finds somebody, they must make a quick evaluation of the condition of the patient. If the victim is alive, they need to decide the best way to get the injured person out. The odds are that the victim will be dragged out and, at the same time, kept closest to the most available oxygen supply. Although firefighters are depicted sharing their source of air, they are taught not to. Two victims are worse than one. Firefighters, like all rescue professionals, take care of

---

Seeing in the Dark

A hot, new technological tool, a helmet-mounted thermal imaging camera called IRIS, will help rescuers locate a downed victim in a structure fire. Heavy smoke can be blinding, but the IRIS sees through it by sensing temperature differences. IRIS alerts rescuers to an unconscious person or even a closed door and the room beyond that could not be seen.

---

themselves. If they do not, they are out of work.

As they work inside a structure, the warning bell on their SCBA gear might jingle. This means they must exit immediately. If they cannot, there is only one option. They can take the air hose that enters the air bottle and stick it deep within their protective clothing. Generally there is a small store of air not contaminated by smoke. That air may be the difference between life and death.

Firefighters who run into burning buildings to save lives themselves have a statistically shortened life. Firefighting is among the most dangerous jobs in the nation and the first responders are at the greatest risk.

Equipment

All equipment relating to rescue is designed to keep the firefighter alive so she can do the job she has to do. Starting from the ground up, turnout gear consists of:

- Steel-toed rubber boots
- Canvaslike bunker pants, made of Nomex, a nonflammable material
- Red suspenders buttoned to the waist, then stored out to the side of the bunker pants, which in turn are pushed down over the boots
- A Nomex heavy, waterproof jacket with reflective markings and buckling closures
- Leather work gloves
- SCBA bottles, valve and face mask
- PASS alert, a warning device attached to the SCBA that rings loudly whenever there has been no movement for five seconds.

Firefighters have been known to forget to turn it on or off. The purpose of PASS is to PASS lead help to the firefighter who is down.

- A Nomex balaclava hood that protects the ears, part of the face and neck
- A helmet with a plastic face shield and Nomex liner, further protecting the ears and neck. A moon-shaped designation will indicate rank or cross-training such as PARAMEDIC. The peculiar shape of the helmet is historic. When made of leather, they were shaped to reinforce the top of the helmet, protecting the top of the head. The back brim was designed to keep water from going down the collar.
- A flashlight mounted on the helmet
- Lengths of rope for marking the way in and out, and for lowering
- Twelve feet of Nylon webbing to convert into an emergency seat
- Forcible entry, commonly called a Halligan tool after the manufacturer
- A grease pencil to indicate rooms that have already been searched or contain bodies
- Wooden door wedges, so workers do not get shut in
- A name tag or identifying number clipped to the turnout gear. When entering and exiting a building, this identification is charted.
- A truck belt for emergency self-rescue, for hanging tools, and for clipping on when performing ladder work

There is a new cutting-edge breathing apparatus containing a mask-mounted, light-sensitive LED display giving a continuous readout of air and mask pressure. Both the firefighter wearing it and the firefighters around her can know whether her air pressure, mask pressure and other functions are okay.

Language

When firefighters are "putting the wet to the red," they have a lexicon of special language. But smoke dampens sound and the roar

The firefighter's most important tools of entry: The firefighter on the left holds a Halligan tool; the one on the right holds an axe. (Photo used by permission of Harvey Eisner.)

Firefighters in full gear. Note the gloves, the flashlights slung at their sides, the Nomex waterproof jackets and boots. They are holding pike poles, also called "hooks," which are used for pulling down doors, walls and windows. (Photo used by permission of Harvey Eisner.)

This firefighter wears an SCBA valve and facemask. (Photo used by permission of Harvey Eisner.)

Old-Timers, New Gear

Old-timers in the fire service, and there are many of them, spend a lot of time grumbling about all this new safety equipment. It's hot, cumbersome and expensive for small departments to purchase. Plus, its use is mandated by the Occupational Safety and Health Administration (OSHA). The fire service is full of stories about fines levied because one firefighter entered a building without a respirator, or a pump operator took his turnout coat off one hot day.

Underlying all this talk is one genuine concern. Fire scenes are intrinsically confused. With all of the smoke, there is little or no visibility, and sounds are often muffled or masked by the noise of pumping equipment. The one reliable sense was touch. In particular, veterans will tell you that the tips of their ears were their temperature sensors. If the structure was getting superheated, close to flashover, then the burning of their ears would tell them to back out quickly.

All of the new turnout gear protects firefighters, but it deprives them of their final reliable sensation about the fire. Ears in particular are now covered by Nomex hoods and ear flaps that are part of the helmet liners. Arguably, firefighters are now better protected, but they are less able to judge the stage of the fire and, thus, are more at risk.

of the flames overwhelms any other noise. So fire rescue in a burning building is conducted largely without words. Communication is limited to hand gestures, pokes and tugs.

Fire departments have a written set of signals to mark rooms searched or containing bodies. For example, a square might indicate the room has been swept and if there were two bodies within, two ×s would be written in the box. This would be drawn low down on the door; that is the working environment.

Radios, often the great hope for communication, get wet in the fire scene and fail.

Dangers

If a firefighter runs out of air, cyanide and carbon monoxide gases will kill. These two are the noxious by-products of the combustion of modern-day synthetic home furnishings. Most people who die in fires are asphyxiated, not burned. The burning comes later, after death.

There are firefighters/rescuers, usually volunteer or call responders in nonurban systems, who have a lack of respect for a fire and usually have never fought a serious fire. There is new meaning to the phrase "baptism by fire." Anyone who isn't aware of the dangers of fire is going to be dangerous to others. Even those who are respectful can become cocky as the fire uses up available oxygen, leaving less for the firefighter's brain. This leaves her feeling goofy, not mentating well. This happens to the experienced pro and is exacerbated by the intense heat, sound and unpredictability of large fires.

Back draft leading to flashover is another danger. Fire in a confined space gets starved for oxygen, so it starts sucking smoke and gases back into the fire, resulting in a back draft. This process also pulls heat back into the fire. In a working fire, back draft can be seen and heard; smoke gets sucked back through windows and under doors, and the scene becomes eerily quiet. Flashover occurs when the superheated combustible materials, solids and gases are exposed to oxygen and explode into flames.

The possibility of a crushing injury is always present when a structure is on fire. Burning buildings collapse. They can fall onto the rescuer, or the rescuer can fall through fire-weakened parts of the building.

Firefighters collapse too. After long sedentary periods at the fire house, the alarm goes off and they face a sudden burst of physically taxing activity in an oxygen-starved setting. Even the most physically fit firefighter is not always ready (and today's urban fire stations have weight rooms available to on-duty crews), and a heart attack or myocardial infarction is not uncommon in response to this sudden demand.

In response to these dangers, fire departments have a two-bottle limit on SCBA activity for men and women entering a fire. After two bottles are used, there is a mandatory physical check done by medics and EMTs. This monitoring of firefighters is called *fire rehab*. Baseline blood pressure readings, pulse and respirations taken prior to the fire are available to be compared to on-scene readings. The medical personnel also have oxygen available. They are on the lookout for dehydration and hyperthermia. (See the Appendix: Rescue Maladies.). When a medical staff member determines a firefighter cannot reenter the building for medical reasons, the firefighter is done for the day.

Other job hazards include falls from the twenty-foot firehouse poles and fire truck crashes, both of which are not uncommon. On the fire ground (the area of the fire), firefighters routinely end up breathing more smoke and gas than they should, and many now face the slow, cumulative effects of smoke inhalation, resulting in respiratory ailments like bronchitis and emphysema. Finally, a searching firefighter faces the real possibility of electrocution by coming into contact with burned-bare but still live electrical wires.

Ambulances are routinely dispatched to structure fires, even those known to have no victims. The medical responders are there for the firefighters.

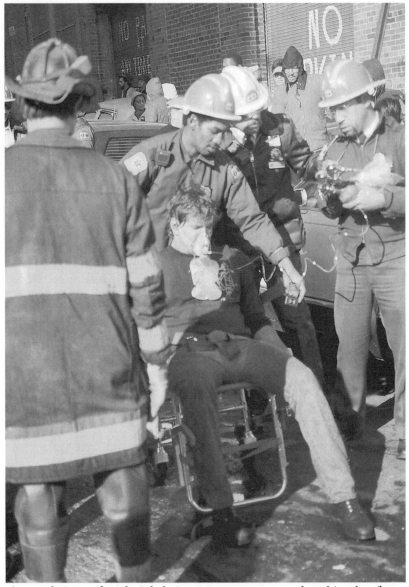

A rescued victim of smoke inhalation wears an oxygen mask and is taken from the scene in a stairchair. (Photo used by permission of Harvey Eisner.)

CHAPTER SIX

Extrication Specialist

People get entangled and stuck in awkward places, often with serious or life-threatening injuries. When vehicles crash at high speeds, the metal of the car body and frame bends upon impact, trapping legs. Children climb into wells. In large structures that collapse, those inside are liable to be trapped under tons of debris. Trenches and excavations in unstable soils often fall in on workers.

These types of disasters present rescuers with a common problem: How can they disentangle the victim(s) without further injury and ensure he'll be alive after withdrawal? The answer is extrication, the rescue science of getting people out of tight spots so that medical responders have access to them. Extrication is a sub-specialty of firefighting. It is one of those fire activities that helped to fill the void as the incidence of structure fires dropped. Today urban departments have a specialized extrication team. In less-populated areas, communities might support a volunteer extrication team. Sometimes several towns might share a team that provides this service to the citizens of all the communities.

These teams work somewhere between EMS and fire as they access and extricate a victim. Their most common focus is getting people out of vehicular crashes.

History of the Profession

Getting stuck, trapped or snared is not a new concept. Humans (along with other animals) have always managed to get themselves into jams. The problem is that the predicaments keep getting more complicated. The history of extrication as a rescue specialty has paralleled the growing complexity of obstructions. As the bottle-necks became more varied and perplexing, tools were invented and fabricated to deal with the ever-changing structures and vehicles of civilization.

It used to be that the policeman responding to the scene of an accident was responsible for extrication. If he couldn't open the doors and drag passengers to safety, then extrication meant finding the nearest guy with tools, assembling manpower and proceeding with whatever was necessary to pry someone out. Extrication was a learn-by-doing, catch-as-catch-can activity, finagled differently every time.

By the 1960s, science and technology began to change so rapidly that subspecialties developed and new tools came on line, each of which demanded its own special training and skills. Rescuers learned, often the hard way, that extrication was dangerous for them as well as for the trapped victim.

The evolution of the automobile is an illustration of the developing problem. As recently as ten years ago, cars had steel floors or platforms upon which the rest of the auto was assembled. Steering columns were attached to the dash and anchored to the floor. In a head-on accident, the floor would buckle, driving down dash and steering wheel and trapping the legs of the driver. Freeing pinned-in victims was a question of pulling on the steering column and the dash enough to free lower limbs.

Then along came unibody construction where the roof and floor are designed to be trusses transferring loads to the front and rear. Steering columns were separated from the dash and were meant to be both free-floating and impact-absorbing. Cars still crumpled upon high-speed impact, but they did it differently. Pulling on the steering column and dash no longer worked. Now the most efficient way to free a stuck driver was to cut away the roof and lift the person out.

About the same time that the technique became well-established and the tools were designed for peeling back the roof, some car design changes came along. Cars were now made using space-body construction—lighter materials that couldn't be cut. Air bags also came into existence which, if they didn't deploy during the accident, exploded in the faces of careless rescuers. New impact-absorbing bumpers contained a hydraulic shock absorber system that blew out during car fires, destroying the lower legs of rescuers who were careless enough to stand directly behind a car after the accident.

Vehicle rescue has had to adapt to each of these changes, responding with new tools and new training. No longer is it possible or safe to gather the first five guys you can find and then try to figure out how to get someone out of a wreck. Responders have to be trained professionals. They have to do their jobs with speed and efficiency, all within close proximity to screams and moans of badly injured or dying victims.

Auto racing, especially Indy car racing, was a second avenue leading to improvements and innovation in vehicle extrication. Race cars crashed at excessive speeds, leaving the driver in what was little more than a bomb with wheels. The driver had to be freed swiftly without adding further injury, and the track had to be cleared. These imperatives led to the development of pneumatic- and hydraulic-powered cutting and spreading devices, and to the creation of medical extrication devices, which can be swiftly applied to secure spinal stabilization while the patient is yanked from the wreck.

Across the country, fire departments have learned from auto racing experiences. Today most departments either cross-train firefighters in rescue techniques and tools, or they have an affiliated company/rescue team that gets called upon when extrication is needed. Larger, urban fire departments have adopted specialized rescue companies with their own rescue truck and are centrally based, responding to calls throughout the service district twenty-four hours a day.

Heavy or collapsed-building rescue had the same spurt of growth and professionalization. The impetus for such changes has been less in response to technological improvements and more in response to bombs, engineering miscalculations and natural catastrophes powerful enough to bring down entire buildings, such as earthquakes, mudslides, volcanic eruptions, hurricanes and tornados.

The history of such heavy rescue is a chronicle of adaptation. Out of necessity, tools for vehicle rescue were adapted to work within collapsed buildings. Construction tools were selected and specialized to accomplish the careful destruction and removal that is critical to this form of rescue. High technology was designed to aid rescuers especially in the fields of locating trapped victims and stabilizing collapsed, potentially unsafe buildings.

Again it is fire departments which, in their quest to keep their personnel employed, have assumed the lead in collapse rescue. While there are instances of separate extrication teams, perhaps affiliated with an ambulance service, usually fire oversees heavy rescue. City rescue trucks carry available gear for building extraction along with their vehicle disentanglement equipment. Rescuers are trained and drilled in both specialties and, in practice, there are crossover skills between vehicular and heavy rescue.

The origin of trench rescue lies in the dawning recognition that construction workers were losing their lives while digging utility trenches. Sadly, would-be rescuers were losing their lives as frequently as the original victims. The federal government, collecting data through OSHA, has been the principal catalyst in trench rescue development.

A cubic yard of earth, $3' \times 3' \times 3'$, weighs three thousand pounds. On average, utility trenches are three feet wide, two to three times as deep and any number of yards long. Unstable soils, rain, groundwater, sudden or continuous vibration from the operation of heavy equipment and carelessness have all combined to spell disaster for trench workers, electricians, pipe fitters or plumbers who "hop into the trench for a quick job." When the trench sides collapse, the soils are entrapping and suffocating. Oftentimes, the scrambling to get out compounds the problem and brings down more soil. It has been estimated that the odds are 500:1 of a secondary collapse, bringing materials into the trench and on top of the victim and rescue workers.

More commonly, the buried are out of sight and left with only a brief supply of air. They have to be dug out before their pocket of air is depleted, which is largely done with hand tools. There is too much risk for injury to the victim otherwise.

Fire department responders are also the ones trained in trench rescue. Rescue trucks carry gear to stabilize trenches so that rescuers, firefighters and construction workers can work safely in the trench and dig out the trapped victim. Perhaps because it appears so simple, trench rescue is one of the most dangerous of the rescue operations.

Education and Certification

Fire academies and fire attack schools have, as part of their curriculum, vehicle, trench and heavy extrication. These courses are entry-level programs for all beginning or probational firefighters. Alternatively, these courses exist for experienced personnel who, by choice or assignment, have become specialists in particular areas and will be in charge of specific rescue scenes.

There are several schools of national repute. The first formal extrication training was formed in the 1970s in Bellmead, Texas, and was followed by the Georgia Extrication School and another school in Sunnyvale, California. There is also an annual event and symposium called the International Vehicle Extrication and Learning Symposium.

The best and most frequent classroom for vehicle extrication is the local automobile junkyard. Fire departments arrange with these junkyards to have individuals or teams come out and practice extrication skills on real cars. Punching out glass, cutting posts and peeling the roof, prying open doors, slicing through side panels—all are skills that benefit from repetition. Practicing on a variety of vehicles allows rescuers to understand how particular makes and models react to an assortment of maneuvers. In addition, systematically destroying junked cars can be strangely satisfying, even therapeutic.

Extrication skills also are taught by the tool manufacturers, who will provide training to those purchasing their products. This training is on-site and led by manufacturer's reps.

There is a growing number of private technical rescue schools that teach particular skills and curricula, and regional and national rescue extrication seminars are a source of continuing education.

A good instructor will acknowledge that he always learns something from each batch of students. Instruction in the use of power

Insider Information

Your well-run extrication team will appoint someone small as interior rescuer. This is the person who readies the scene from inside out so that the extrication can move along in a timely fashion. It is this extrication specialist who notices that the brake handle penetrating the driver's thigh will have to be removed before the victim is going anywhere. If you write into your story an interior rescuer, be sure she keeps the following checklist in mind, as suggested from *Rescue* Magazine, now called *Fire Rescue*:

- Wear full gear and goggles.
- Carry a radio.
- Bring a blanket roll inside with you.
- Be sure the vehicle is fully stabilized before entering.
- Gain access.
- Check for flammable liquids.
- Remember to communicate with the rest of the team outside.
- Take lighting with you.
- Roll down the windows.
- Unlock all of the doors.
- Cut the seat belts.
- Tilt/telescope the steering wheel.
- Secure the air bag.
- Slide the seat back.
- Lower the seat.
- Check all knobs and pedals.
- Turn off the ignition.
- Update command.
- Notify EMS of the victim's condition.

tools goes on side by side with the encouragement of innovation and creativity; each incident these learning rescuers will encounter will hold a new set of challenges. A piece of the education will be full-blown scenarios, often with live victims and medical providers.

Job Description

In outline form, these three rescue fields depend upon the same organizing principles or action plan. And, as with all rescue, when the situation overtaxes immediately available resources, the ICS is put into effect.

The rescuer's first task when he arrives on-scene is to size up the site and the anticipated operations. How is the rescue going to be accomplished? What supplies and manpower will be needed? Then the rescuer in charge has to identify all present and anticipated obstacles and hazards. This is an exercise that asks the questions: What are the worst things that can go wrong with this scene and, if they happen, how are we going to deal with them? These rescues are loaded with dangers for victim and rescuer alike. The way to deal with and control the dangers is to identify what the dangers are before they become a problem and expose the team. These planning decisions have to be made in split seconds. That's where experience and thorough training come into play. Once the scene is sized up, plans are made and threats are at least identified, then it's time to go to work.

For vehicle extrication, the plan is to free the trapped victim as quickly as possible. Usually this means destroying whatever may be left of the post-crash automobile. Side posts are cut, the top is peeled back like an opened sardine can, and dash and steering wheel are pried out of the way.

The first step in establishing access is to make sure that the truck or auto is stable in whatever position it landed. Whether right side up, upside down or on its side, the vehicle must be shored up, blocked and stabilized so that it cannot move and trap or pin the unwary rescuer. A variety of tools accomplish this. Rescue trucks carry odd-length pieces of wood and timbers that can be wedged under the car or built up like Lincoln Logs to form a stabilizing pier. Ropes and cables can be used to tie off the vehicle. Air bags, the newest pieces of rescue equipment, can also be used. They are placed under strategic points and then inflated by a compressor or even by SCBA air bottles. They can develop tremendous pounds-per-square-inch (PSI) lifting force and, with careful siting, provide a stable platform for the now-lifted vehicle.

Next, access to the passenger compartment is accomplished by breaking out the windows. Rescuers carry a spring-loaded metal punch that accomplishes this in seconds, breaking the safety glass into harmless, snowlike shards. At this point if not before, medical providers enter the car and initiate whatever care is possible in the confined space. Simultaneously, rescuers double-check to be certain the ignition is off and any automatic devices such as air bags have been disarmed. For safety's sake, a careful rescuer cuts the battery cables to make sure no electrical current is in the car. Finally, before beginning heavy cutting and lifting, the victim and medical providers within the car are covered with a blanket or tarp heavy enough to keep them from getting further injured by bits of glass, metal or sparks.

The strength of a car lies in the posts that connect the two trusses on the top and the floor. Frequently, the only way to open the passenger compartment is to open the roof. This procedure requires cutting the "A post" on both sides of the windshield. Then the rescuer cuts the "B post" just behind the front doors. These four cuts are usually sufficient to allow the roof to be rolled back, opening the inside. If not, two final cuts are made on the posts to either side of the rear window, after which the entire roof can be lifted away and the rescuer can assess interior strategies.

Severing the posts can be accomplished with a variety of saws, but is most quickly done by using a hydraulically or pneumatically driven tool that can deliver as much as 30,000 PSI cutting force. The Hurst Tool, which weighs a heavy thirty pounds and must be held up in the air while it does its work, has been the standard for so long that rescuers frequently talk about the Hurst Tool even when the instrument is manufactured by someone else. This noisy alligatorlike cutter is powered by a compressor built into the rescue truck. It is usually gasoline-driven and is set up near the wreck. In short order, the rescue scene is covered with a tangle of hose lines running from compressors to a variety of air- or fluid-driven tools.

This cutting tool is like a pair of blunt, power-driven scissors. The titanium blades are no more than three or four inches long. Once they get proper purchase, they slowly but inevitably pinch their way through posts, hinges and reinforcements. A variety of hand tools, pry bars and the like will have first been used to expose the structural components to be cut. As the cutting edges are on either side of the target, the operator slowly increases pressure and waits for the tool to do its work.

Once the roof has been removed and the doors opened, if the victim still is not withdrawn, the rescuer might switch to another popular and effective power-driven tool. The spreader uses the same power source as the cutter, but the force opens rather than closes its jaws. Depending upon the size of the tool inserted, a spreader can expand a tiny area to several inches, or expand a ten-inch gap to double the size. Spreaders are the tool of choice to pry crumbled dashboards off of pinned legs. The public knows this tool as the "jaws of life." Within the profession, it is called "the jaws." To help the spreaders get started, a variety of small pry bars, Halagan tools and jacks are used to create openings. As openings are created, blocks and cribbing hold apart what has been gained and eliminate metal falling back on the victim or rescuer.

Once the jaws have had a chance to work, the victim is freed from the car. Removal of the roof and all four doors from a car will have taken a skilled team ten minutes. Medical providers will then straighten out the pretzeled body, but at least all pinning metal is gone. Access has been established.

Collapsed-building or heavy rescue is similar to vehicle extrication, except the scale is larger. The same cutting, lifting and shoring tools are used, but they are bigger or there must be more of them. Heavy rescuers working in collapsed structures cut paths to their subjects. These professionals use saws that would not be appropriate if they were right next to or above the victim, like chain saws for timbers and wooden construction, and circular saws with diamond blades for concrete and masonry construction. Air chisels dut-dut-dut their way through masonry. Heavy equipment such as bulldozers, backhoes and cranes, and professional operators may be recruited to remove and push aside rubble.

As access is cut in, cribbing or staging follows every step, stabilizing the wrecked building. This is slow, heavy and dangerous work—definitely not for the fainthearted.

Collapsed-building rescues can take days and, on occasion, even weeks as air, food and emotional support are supplied to the victims. Usually, however, most rescues turn into body recoveries. It is not uncommon for rescuers who have labored for days—always in good communication with an apparently healthy victim—to finally reach him, heave the last 600-pound slab of concrete to the side to free his pinned legs, and then have the object of their Herculean efforts collapse and die in their arms due to a medical phenomenon known as *crush syndrome*. (See the Appendix: Rescue Maladies.)

The world of the heavy rescuer is dangerous and frustrating. It's like crawling through a house of cards: Your character will be tempted to hold her breath to make sure she doesn't accidentally jostle the structure. But in fact the rescuer cannot be quiet or still. To the contrary, she operates heavy tools and moves massive amounts of rubble in a dark, smoke- or dust-filled environment. Radios usually don't work inside a collapsed structure, so communication is sketchy. Usually she'll move on hands and knees or belly, clawing her way forward in what she hopes is the right direction, dragging tools and supplies behind. (Female heavy rescuers are particularly useful when space is minimal.) Even as she forges forward, she plans her way out. Her greatest worry is a secondary collapse that will seal her in, instantly changing her from rescuer to another trapped victim.

The world of the trench rescuer is clear and usually in the daylight. Most of what she does is make sure that no more disintegration occurs. This is accomplished by shoring up the still-intact sides with paneling and bracing, something the contractor should have been doing in the first place. Only after the trench is soundly stabilized is it safe to go in and start digging to free the trapped victim.

The world of the trench rescuer is usually not fun-filled. Because it takes time to stabilize the sides, your trench victim will probably be dead from the crushing weight or from asphyxiation.

Actual digging in the trench must be slow and careful, and by hand. It is too easy to stumble upon the body where you least expect it and do inadvertent damage. There is a trench rescue tool that works like a giant vacuum and is capable of moving large volumes of loose soil in rapid order without threatening the well-being of the victim, but few departments have this expensive device.

Equipment

The tools of extrication are the instruments of lifting, moving, cutting and stabilizing. Rarely are they delicate, small or precise. They can get the job done with security for rescuer and victim alike. Because the rescue tools for extrication are used in assorted settings for a multiplicity of purposes, they all are carried in the same rescue truck.

Vehicle extrication demands a wide assortment of stabilization gear such as blocks, jacks, cribbing, ropes, cable, air bags—anything that will make sure the vehicle will not move again until the rescuers are ready to move it. A compressor is also necessary to power the cutters and spreaders (the jaws) and the air pillows.

The air tools themselves have a conglomeration of jaws and cutters sized for particular applications and openings. Then there is a large assortment of hand tools designed to punch out auto glass, smash door locks, pierce holes in sheet metal giving access to the cutters, and cut an assortment of metals, plastics and composite fibers now found in car construction.

Heavy or collapsed-building rescue demands all of the above plus an assortment of saws to cut through wood and masonry. There will be an interesting collection of instrumentation—microphones, cameras, fiber-optic devices, infrared sensors, seismic instruments—designed to listen for sounds of life deep inside a collapsed building, to sense the heat of life and to detect minuscule vibrations and movements. Collapse rescuers will take an air hose into the building that not only supplies oxygen but also marks their way out. If oxygen inside the building is not a problem, they will uncoil a rope or "tag line" behind them to show them the way home. If they cannot uncoil an oxygen line but do need a fresh air supply, they will use redesigned SCBAs that are smaller or mount to the side so they do not hang up in confined spaces.

The significant advances in collapse rescue are small tools such as locating devices that tell rescuers if someone is still alive inside and pinpoints where they are. Heat-sensing, acoustical, seismic and fiber-optic tools have all been enlisted to help in a search. Sensitive engineering instruments tell rescuers if there have been minute shifts in the building or if everything is still stable. Compressors, fans and an assortment of air delivery systems are used to keep both rescuers and victims supplied with fresh air.

A Clean Cut

An Air Knife and Vacuum has two pneumatic elements, both driven by standard air compressors. Air converted to supersonic speed will break up soil around trapped victims. The vacuum picks up and deposits loose material outside the trench. Both of these chores are accomplished without harming the unhappy victim.

In a vehicular rescue, the safety and security of the victims and rescuers can be enhanced with a thick layer of foam designed to be placed underneath the accident vehicle.

The following list hints at the depth and complexity of the gear carried in a large rescue truck. The availability of purchase funds is the biggest limiting factor. Rescue tools are expensive, and they are still evolving. The bottom line on rescue tools is that there are a number of ways of getting things done. What's important is that your rescue personalities stay calm even when everyone else around them may be losing their heads. They would not try to muscle the job. They would know their heads are their toolboxes and that's the place to look for solutions.

A well-outfitted rescue vehicle carries:

LOCATING EQUIPMENT fiber-optic search scopes, global positioning systems, light amplification (night vision) devices, PASS alarms, seismic/acoustic detection systems, sonar, thermal imaging or infrared devices, video search cameras.

BREATHING EQUIPMENT air cylinders/bottles, diving spare air, escape bottles (emergency small cylinders), filter masks, rebreather system, SCBA and SCUBA, supplied air breathing apparatus (direct line from compressor).

COMMUNICATIONS EQUIPMENT cellular and satellite telephones, communications wire/rope/tag lines, hardwired systems, radio frequency systems.

SOURCES OF POWER FOR EQUIPMENT AND TOOLS batteries, generators, hydraulic pressure, internal combustion engines, pneumatic pressure power.

SPREADING, CUTTING, DRILLING AND IMPACTING DEVICES air knife, alligator spreaders, chisels, cutters, cutting torches, feather and wedge, hand tools, jack hammers, percussive rescue tools, rams, saws.

LIFTING AND PULLING EQUIPMENTS air bags, come-along, expander bolts, high-strength rope, jacks, slings, underwater lifting bags.

SHORING DEVICES air shores, hydraulic shores, lumber, screw shores.

ROPE, RIGGING AND HAULING EQUIPMENT ascenders, brake racks, carabiners, descenders, edge rollers, etriers, guardrail anchor device, harnesses, kern mantel rope, mechanical advantage system, natural fiber rope, portable winches, pulleys, rescue figure eights, Stokes' spiders (webbing to lift a stretcher), tripod, webbing.

ENVIRONMENTAL MONITORING AND DANGEROUS ATMOSPHERE EQUIP- MENT environmental monitors, nonsparking tools, pneumatically powered lights, ventilation fans and ducts.

VICTIM EXTRICATION DEVICES all-terrain stretchers, backboards, immobilization devices, encapsulating litters.

STRUCTURAL MOVEMENT SENSING DEVICES levels, transit, submersible pumps.

MISCELLANEOUS EQUIPMENT nail gun, hand tools.

Language

At the beginnings of rescue from vehicles and buildings, big men using muscle were called upon. These males were perceived as having large bellies. When the Hurst Tool became a common item among rescuers, the term "rescue ledge" for the rescuer's abdomen became common usage. The Hurst Tool is heavy; it tends to be utilized by steadying it against one's rescue ledge.

The dialect of extrication is the language of the tools used. The extrication designation of auto body parts—A, B and C posts—has moved into the common language.

Dangers

The dangers from extrication are the hazards of the unexpected. The overturned auto was not blocked completely, and it shifts just a little when the first medical provider enters. Or the car that burst into flames after the accident turns out to have several cylinders of compressed gas or live ammunition in the trunk that begins to explode.

In a collapsed structure, aside from unanticipated movement, there are the expected but sometimes overlooked perils of loose electrical currents coursing down pipes and wires, or gases leaking from ruptured lines.

The possibilities of rescuer suffocation or poisoning lurk. An explosion triggered by a spark as metal hits metal, or the sparking of an internal combustion engine fired up to power the rescuer's compressor can prove fatal for the extricator.

The danger of trench rescue is instability. Unless you're planning a disaster, don't let your rescuer persona go down there until the trench is secure and the sides are shored. This dictum is difficult to follow because your trapped victim will have just disappeared from sight or will be oh-so-close and about to up-and-die (UAD). There will be little time to accomplish the rescue; the child's air supply may not last the time it takes to set up shoring. Rush, rush, rush.

Wrong, wrong, wrong. The way to accomplish the goal is to slow down, think efficiently, work as a team. Speed can lead to the loss of another life trying to save one that is already gone.

CHAPTER SEVEN

Hazmat Responder

C ave people sitting around a fire knew enough to move when the smoke blew into their faces. The smoke smelled noxious, stung their eyes and in sufficient concentration could produce a hacking cough. Mankind has not lost that innate drive to get away from harmful things. The problem of the 1990s is threefold:

- There are a multitude of substances—solids, liquids and gasses—that are harmful to the environment and to people.
- Many of these substances are invisible, do not have distinctive odors and do their damage without prior notification.
- These substances are widely distributed within the workplace, in the home, on the highways, railways and plane lines. They are, in short, everywhere.

Hazardous materials (hazmat) rescue is the profession that removes the ill, the injured and the threatened from dangerous environments. This must be effected without exposing rescuers to contaminants or risks, and without worsening the situation. To accomplish this, rescuers have to be fully trained hazmat responders capable of recognizing and controlling any spill, providing for the general public safety, cleaning up the spill and, almost coincidentally, removing from the scene those who are already contaminated.

Because the rescuer is as much at risk as the victim, hazmat rescue particularly stresses self-preservation.

History of the Profession

In the late 1950s, a ship carrying ammonium nitrate caught fire at a loading dock in Galveston, Texas. This was a hazmat incident before something called hazmat existed. The fertilizer exploded and killed over five hundred people, completely destroying the dock, other ships and part of the city.

Following this event, accidents involving tankers and railcars were spilling chemicals that spread in puddles or vaporized into clouds of toxic gasses. Nobody knew how to deal with these new emergencies. They were everywhere: in abandoned fields, on farms, on city streets. Throughout the 1950s, 1960s and 1970s, hundreds of victims in industrial, agricultural, private and municipal settings were overcome by toxic fumes while working in enclosed spaces such as sewer systems, pipelines, tunnels, mines and storage tanks.

The one goal was that those caught within the clutch of a dangerous chemical needed to be removed to a safer place. The public and then their legislators became concerned as passersby and trained rescuers were compounding the problem by leaping into the situation and, instead of rescuing, becoming victims themselves.

In 1986, Title 49 of the federal regulations code defined a hazardous material as "any substance or material in a quantity or form which poses an unreasonable risk to health, safety, and property when transported in commerce." Others have defined it as anything jumping from its container when something goes wrong, which hurts or harms the things it touches. These definitions were the first outward appearance of governmental concerns about toxic items, and the first recognition that these materials existed in the world of commerce and industry.

That same legislation required companies to provide information on hazardous materials stored at their sites. This was a start toward protecting not only employees but also emergency responders. The Superfund Law required that all hazmat rescuers be appropriately trained to handle a hazmat incident, though it failed to define "appropriately." Nonetheless, rescuer training was evolving. The dangers of chemical spills and toxic environments would be analyzed and respected.

In 1990, OSHA and the Environmental Protection Agency (EPA) published the original guidelines for hazmat response and created competency levels for hazmat rescuers.

- Level One: Awareness training for citizens who might encounter a hazmat situation.
- Level Two: Operations training, or how to organize a hazmat response.
- Level Three: Technician training to safely perform specific skills.

These levels were the operative levels for responders who would enter the contaminated environment and bring victims out. To accomplish this task, rescuers had to be trained to recognize the dangers, learn how to control them, acquire and be comfortable with appropriate high-tech gear and encapsulating suits, and grasp how to stage victim recovery areas so that both they and the people they retrieved would not spread contamination outside of the original spill.

Since these first steps, hazmat response and rescue have become sophisticated though the principles remain the same. Certainly the incidents are the same. That early Texas event involving the fertilizer was mirrored in the 1990s. It was the same ammonium nitrate that wrecked the federal building in Oklahoma City and took so many lives.

Like extrication, hazmat skills have become the province of local firefighters, sometimes cross-trained along with their other duties, sometimes specially formed into response teams.

One development distinguishing hazmat rescue from other rescue professions is that private industry and the federal government have both created their own twenty-four-hour response teams that can deploy rapidly to anywhere in the country. The Chemical Manufacturer's Association has formed CHEMTREC (Chemical Transportation Emergency Center), which mans an 800 number 365 days a year, ready to respond with advice and assistance in any chemical emergency. The Coast Guard has federal responsibility to monitor and, if necessary, assist in cleanup of major spills. It mans a National Response Center and dispatches National Response Teams (NRT).

A hazmat unit responds to a call. Note that this unit is part of a fire department. (Photo used by permission of Harvey Eisner.)

Hazmat Happenings

Hazmat World: The Magazine for Environmental Management is free. Order it from Hazmat World, P.O. Box 50112, Cicero, IL 60650. (708) 462-2347. This is filled with trends, equipment, services and techniques.

The Hazmat World Literature Guide is a free publication listing other publications, equipment and services. Hazmat World, P.O. Box 3021, Wheaton, IL 60189.

A free hazmat training video and *Dispatch* newsletter is available from Emergency Film Group, 225 Water Street, Plymouth, MA 02360. (800) 842-0999.

Both NRT and CHEMTREC physically respond to large-scale emergencies but for the most part, their involvement is information-gathering and assistance. Your rescuer-character can call either 800 number for information on the level of danger posed by a particular chemical, whether gas, solid or liquid.

Hazmat is a twentieth-century invention. While deleterious substances have been in the air from both natural sources (volcanic ash) and as a result of civilization's needs (coal dust), they were not

---

Confined Space Education

Numerous proprietary concerns offer training, all with names like:

- CMC Rescue School
- Emergency Consulting and Research Center
- Emergency Response Institute
- Emergency Response Training, Inc.
- Emergency Training Consultants
- Mid-Atlantic Rescue Technologies

- Progressive Rescue Solutions
- Rescue Concepts, Inc.
- Rescue 3 International
- Science Applications International
- Spec Rescue International
- START Rescue Training

(Some of the above offer rescue courses other than confined space.)

---

perceived as a problem that could be addressed. With greater and more varied sources of such pollution, it became clear that rescue for those in trouble was essential and manageable.

Education and Certification

The federal government has joined with industry to develop a number of programs in hazmat and hazmat rescue training. There are nine federal educational sites around the country where fire and industry personnel can receive intensive instruction in the several levels of hazmat response. Hazmat teams from big city fire departments, sometimes incorporated into the rescue team and truck, prefer to train on-site. The required skills are confusing and time-consuming and, from an administrative point of view, expensive.

OSHA requires those at risk be certified to some level of hazmat expertise. The bulk of this education is for level one: hazmat awareness. A nonprofessional citizen rescuer trained to level one knows enough to recognize a developing hazmat situation and to clear the scene as rapidly as possible while awaiting professional help.

The second and third levels, operations and technician, are for the professional hazmat rescuers. These responders take an offensive position and control the entire situation. As always in rescue emergencies, when the situation warrants it, initiate the ICS. In addition to identifying, controlling and cleaning up a dangerous hazmat scene, they also decontaminate victims, including themselves, before turning care of the victims over to medical providers.

Rescuers stage a hazmat scene into three distinct areas. The hot zone is where the danger lies whether it is dust, liquid, vapor, gas, solid, mist or runoff. The hot zone is the immediate area of the spill or contamination. If the spill is small, it might be contained in a corner of a room. That is the hot zone, the area of containment. If, however, the spill is a heavy volatile gas blowing from a wrecked railroad car, the hot zone could extend miles downwind from the accident, and everyone caught in its path could be contaminated.

The warm zone is an area safer for responders because it is further removed from the threat. But protective clothing is still necessary. This is where rescuers decontaminate hazmat victims and themselves. Attire and personal possessions are securely bagged. Contaminants are hosed or brushed off, then placed in sealed containers. Finally, remaining residues are neutralized and that residue, too, is sealed.

This procedure is relatively easy if rescuers are concentrating on an acid spill splashed on the pants of a nearby worker. But cleanup is infinitely more difficult if the contaminant coats a city street or is a microscopic, airborne particle which, in small doses, causes cancer. This is why hazmat training at the upper levels of responsibility is so rigorous.

Like firefighters who enter premises where the air is unfit for human consumption, the hazmat rescuer will need to be certified in the use of an SCBA. That bottle of air is all that lies between the rescuer and her own contamination. In some situations, the SCBA gear is worn under the white, totally encasing protective suit to seal the whole system. This is the spacemanlike look that appears in newspaper and magazine photographs and is described in books. The material is Tyvek-like, which is used to wrap houses to eliminate wind infiltration; it has the ability to breathe outwardly, without admitting any air movement from the exterior. Nonetheless, these suits are hot and confining.

Hazmat rescue is necessary in wells and pipes where the air is compromised. If the victim is in a confined space with a very narrow

On the fringe of a "warm zone" hazmat responders place contaminants into bags, which are sealed. (Photo used by permission of Harvey Eisner.)

What's in a Trench?

A trench is a narrow excavation in the ground that is deeper than it is wide. A trench is also a confined space and should be treated as such. Although it is illegal under OSHA standards to enter a four-foot or deeper trench unless it has been shored, construction crews do so. It is costly to shore up a trench, and the usual repsonse by employees after a collapse is, "But I was only going to be in there for a minute!"

These disasters are compounded when a bystander enters the trap to rescue the first victim, and both are imprisoned by a secondary collapse.

---

opening, the SCBA gear will not fit in along with the rescuer. In this circumstance, the rescuer will be certified to work with an air line running from a compressor to her face mask.

Qualifications

A hazmat rescuer is in good physical and mental health. This work is physically and emotionally draining. The breathing apparatus and the rescue suits are hot. Even short periods of work in full regalia can be exhausting. Conditioning is rechecked regularly.

Tests are given to ensure this professional has no respiratory weakness. Your hazmat responder should not be drawn as claustrophobic as he dons all of his safety gear and is lowered into a dark, three-foot-wide hole some fifteen feet deep. This type of hazmat rescue, into a confined space, has another set of difficulties along with the hazmat aspects. The responder must be able to negotiate small black areas by feel as he keeps his head and continues to concentrate on his victim.

In confined space rescue, the victim is most often already dead from lack of oxygen. The rescuer needs the fortitude to deal with that disappointment after working hard to try and save the trapped individual.

Job Description

The agenda of hazmat rescue is to go in and get the victim, to decontaminate everyone as they retreat from the hot zone and to endeavor to contain the spill in the smallest possible, secure area. This work is painstaking.

Because numerous hazmat incidents occur in confined spaces, the rescuer must be familiar with rope and rigging systems, and safe, fast body retrieval. The speed is necessary for the rescuer's safety. As it is, 60 percent of Americans who die in confined spaces are the rescuers. Usually they have risked their own lives to conduct body recoveries, although they often do not know this at the onset.

Whether a confined space rescue or an open hazardous material leak, the rescuer's problem is her air supply. She must respect the dangerous environment she has to enter and work within, not try to conquer it.

Equipment

Aluminum foil-like suits or white Tyvek plastic protective suits that protect the body from contaminants as well as reflecting heat are the garb for your hazmat responder. Either suit must be completely leakproof. Putting them on is a slow process because helpers must tape every seam. Sometimes the suits have an SCBA system under them; others are connected by an umbilicus to a constant fresh air supply; still others have flexible ductwork attached at the back that is used to inflate the suit, providing positive pressure to stop infiltration, and as a breathing supply.

Atmospheric monitors and sensors will be used for both large-scale and confined space hazmat rescue. It is essential for the rescuer to know exactly where the contamination is and how concentrated it is.

For the cleanup in the warm zone, hazmat rescuers will need a variety of tarps, cleaning agents, buckets, bags and barrels to remove, catch and securely package all contaminants.

There are special low-profile stretchers and half-size backboards meant to get victims out of tight spots. Often these are used in combination with webbing and ropes designed to package and lift out the victim.

The main concern about equipment on a hazmat scene is contamination, or that the chemicals themselves may ruin gear. Equipment that enters the hot zone often never returns into

This hazmat specialist wears an insulated, leak-proof suit for protection against the contaminant being stored in the drum. Note the SCBA system worn strapped to the back beneath the suit. (Photo used by permission of Harvey Eisner.)

service, so in addition to all of its other problems, hazmat rescue is a major consumer of equipment.

Responders going down into holes where radios and cell phones don't work will have hardwired communication systems and will wear a headset. Their escape will be insured by a rescue/entry tripod. This three-legged system sits over the hole, and adjusts from six to ten feet in height.

Lights are an important piece of equipment when the hazmat incident is in a confined space. There are all sorts of illuminating devices, ranging from tripod systems to large generators with light kits built in.

Kendrick Extrication Device (KED), a form of spine splint, might be utilized to remove a victim from a confined space who might have an injured spine. This vestlike immobilizer allows access to the front of the torso so the lungs can be auscultated with a stethoscope, and carotid veins in the neck—good trauma indicators for chest injuries—can be seen. While the KED stabilizes the backbone, it does not inhibit breathing and is a replacement for a long board and straps, which could not be used within a boat's hold, for example. The KED keeps the body's trunk straight while the legs are free.

Language

BSI Body substance isolation, or protection from vomitus, feces, urine, saliva and blood of others.

IDLH Immediately dangerous to life and health.

MSDS Materials safety data sheets, which are required to accompany the storage or transport of any hazardous materials.

NFPA National Fire Protection Association, the author of numerous standards for hazmat response.

PLACARD An identifying sign required on all vehicles containing hazmat.

ROUTE OF EXPOSURE Inhaled through the lungs or absorbed through the skin: how a chemical affects human body systems.

UN/NA/PIN Three choices of universal names—United Nations, North American, personal identification number—given to a chemical so everyone is talking about the same substance.

Confined Space Trailer Inventory

Fire Rescue magazine ran a story on a rescue involving eighty-eight fire and EMS personnel from eight fire departments who worked together during a five-hour operation. The article includes the following list of gear that was available to the rescuers:

- 23″ to 36″ airshores
- 42″ to 66″ airshores
- 2″×10″×10′ beams
- 4″×4″×10′ beams
- 6″×6″×10′ beams
- 2″ steel pipe, 10′
- air cart for airshores
- backboard
- caution tape
- chain saw
- complete air line systems
- duct tape
- electric fan
- extension cords
- five-gallon buckets
- full-body harnesses
- generator
- gerry cans
- gloves
- goggles
- hammers
- hand rakes
- hand tree saws
- hand winches
- jacks and handles
- jumpsuits
- kernmantle rope
- laminated trench panels with strong backs
- manila rope
- mattock
- nylon rope
- panel cheater bar
- pivot bases for airshores, three
- plywood ground pads
- portable lights
- posthole digger
- potato hoes
- roof ladder
- SAR helmets
- screwjacks, six
- shovels, short and long-handled
- spade
- steel cable straps
- steel spikes
- Stokes litter basket
- support jacks
- tape measure
- traffic cones
- two-wheel dolly
- two-wheel cart for tools or soil
- victim escape bottle
- wedges
- wheel chocks
- winches and tripod
- workbelt
- wristlets

Dangers

Hazmat rescuers can't allow themselves to be exposed to the same contaminants that downed their victims. Depending upon the cause of the incident, their skin and lungs must be fully protected. If there is no way to avoid this, then they keep away. And in real life, they do.

Rescuers apply a Kendrick Extrication Device to immobilize and extricate a victim. The device secures the victim's head, neck and torso. (Photos used by permission of Ferno-Washington.)

Confined space rescue seems to be what gets most rescuers into trouble. No doubt your character might know better but nonetheless will enter a manhole to try to pull out a worker he can see but cannot reach. He might discover too late that the original problem was caused by an unexpected concentration of carbon monoxide, invisible and odorless, lying in wait for whomever ventured down. Too often, then, additional rescuers who should have known better drop down the manhole to rescue their buddy and they, too, succumb. Hazmat rescuers must all be sure the air they breathe is monitored and protected. The danger here is compassion: caring to the point where imprudent risks are taken.

Explosion, fire, suffocation, late development of cancers, poisoning and skin contamination are dangers inherent in this work.

CHAPTER EIGHT

Water Rescuer

Water is not a natural environment for human life. It can become an agent causing immediate, life-threatening situations. It can be dangerous in its passive role. When a canoe tips in a turbulent river and the current sweeps the paddler downstream, the rescue is defined as a swiftwater one. But if it's not the water that is actively challenging life, such as when a victim is working to keep from drowning, an open water rescue will be performed.

Swiftwater rescue occurs most commonly in fast-moving rivers and streams. However, tidal rips and undertows along the edges of oceans and large lakes, along with floodwaters rampaging down city streets and drainage structures, are also the stuff of this type of operation. Rescuers battle the force of the flowing water in their efforts to reach and pull the victim to safety.

In contrast, open or deep water rescue is a race against duration rather than against the thrust of moving waters. When a swimmer is in distress in open water, a race ensues between his strength to stay afloat and the time it takes to remove him from the water.

Rescuers can expect to practice their deep water rescue skills in bodies of water—ponds, lakes and oceans—and in quarries, gravel pits, swimming pools and, for a subspecialty of water rescue called dive rescue, under the water's surface.

History of the Profession

There are few people who make their living exclusively as water rescuers. There are lots of rescue professionals who are trained in water rescue as well as other rescue specialties. Certainly there are skills used in water rescue that carry over to other rescue areas, such as rope work.

In this water rescue scene, the victim grabs a throwline and is pulled to the safety of the boat. The rescuer remains in the boat unless it becomes clear the victim is incapable of being rescued with the rope. (Photo © CMC Rescue, Inc., used by permission.)

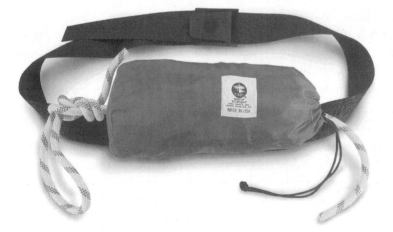

The rescuer in the scene above is using a patrol throwline bag that is strapped to his waist. Here's a closer look at the bag, which functions like a fanny pack, allowing the rescuer to keep both hands free. (Photo © CMC Rescue, Inc., used by permission.)

Open or deep water rescue has its origins in coastal lifesaving stations and manned lighthouses. Wherever shoals, tides, rocks and currents conspired to create ship graveyards, rescue crews were available around the clock to launch lifeboats, rescuing those in distress on ships. The process was dangerous because most calls of distress were due to bad weather. The lifeboat crews would launch their open boats. Six men frantically rowed through surf and storm surge. They would pull from the water any passengers or crew members they could find. Or they maneuvered to the hulls of sinking or stranded ships and loaded human cargo.

The return trip to safety, now heavily weighted down or even worse, overloaded, could be more treacherous than the foray out.

If the lifesaving boats could not be put to sea and if the failing vessel were close to shore, driven onto the rocks, there was an alternative. A rope would be fired or thrown across the stranded ship and a breeches buoy rigged. In calm weather, this canvas sling or chair with a flotation ring to either step into or sit upon was used to exchange crew and cargo between ships at sea. In rough seas, once a rope was extended from ship mast to shore, the buoy system could transport passengers and ship's company above the snarling seas to safety on shore. A tag line, tied to the chair and the ship, could haul the buoy back out for the next refugee.

It is a miracle that anyone—boat passengers, crew, lifesavers—survived these daring feats. They were accomplished at the height of a storm and often in the middle of the night from a ship that was breaking up as it pounded against boulder-lined shores. Yet many did. Newspapers of the day were full of the exploits of crews and individual lighthouse keepers who risked their lives to effect coastal rescues. Stark, black-and-white etchings by Winslow Homer capture the drama and the danger.

Through the 1800s and early 1900s, coastal schooners navigated within sight of land by feeling their way along the shores and only occasionally risking a straight-line course over deep water between two points. If the land was their frame of reference, it was also their downfall.

Today the risk of coastal sinking is minimal. Modern navigational tools such as radar, sonar, GPS (global positioning system) and lo-

---

Coast Guard Procedures

When a Mayday call is received, the closest Coast Guard station responds. All other traffic is instructed to switch to an alternate distress channel, saving that one frequency for the dispatcher and the Mayday caller.

In a clipped, calm, *reassuring* voice, the dispatcher identifies himself each time he is to speak. "This is Coast Guard Station, Woods Hole, Massachusetts Group." Then he works through a carefully conceived set of questions. In the event transmission is lost, the first several questions on the list have to do with location, identification of the vessel and number of people on board including their ages. The dispatcher will then direct that personal float devices (PFDs) be donned and will ask if flares are available. Dispatch will want to know if anyone is injured or has pertinent medical history.

Due to costs, both financial and human, Mayday calls are serious business. False Mayday alerts are punishable with imprisonment and huge fines, commensurate with the costs involved with an unnecessary response, often involving helicopters and ships.

---

ran, and the size and strength of steel ships keep them well off shore and out of harm's way.

Because of the lack of need, there is no contemporary provision for the rescue of ships driven ashore. Lifesaving stations with their rowing crews are a piece of history. Lighthouses are no longer manned by a keeper and his family; many have been closed, judged no longer necessary for coastal navigational purposes. Automated lights and foghorns rule the day.

Today the United States Coast Guard is the professional rescuer on the high seas, in the Great Lakes and on the major rivers of commerce. The USCG is stationed at points up and down the shores of all navigable waters. "Mayday; Mayday" (a corruption of the French *m'aidez* or "help me"), the universally recognized radio distress call, will bring a response from the Coast Guard.

Lifeguarding

As improvements to ships and shipping moved commerce away from the dangers of the shore, other developments produced new shoreline risks. Improvements in public transportation in the 1800s made it possible for the masses to enjoy a Sunday's bathing at the beach. As the public discovered swimming and relaxation upon the shores, cities felt the need to provide lifeguards. Working from spotting towers as they surveyed the swimmers, these intrepid young men stroking through the water or responding in boats would rush to the aid of those in trouble, pulling them from the water and hopefully out of harm's way.

Over the years, lifeguarding developed its own particular patterns of rescue, some for exhausted or cramped swimmers in deep water, others for rescues out of swiftwater in currents and undertows along the shore. New tools evolved to help make the process safer for the rescuer. Various combinations of ropes, buoys and flotation devices could be thrown to the struggling subject. Lifeguards rushed out with buddy boards capable of supporting two people. More recently, mechanical aids like motorboats and wave riders have come into play.

Almost from its outset, lifeguard rescue was driven by one tenet. A terrified, about-to-drown swimmer was a serious danger to her rescuer. In an effort to stay above water, victims were known to grab onto and submerge their lifesavers. For this reason, almost all shoreside rescues were driven by the maxim: Reach/Throw/Row/Go. Following its meaning, the safest deep water rescue is accomplished by never leaving land and extending out a stick or hand to the subject. The next best choice is tossing a rope and hauling the victim in. The third option is going out in a boat to accomplish the rescue. The final option, both the worst pick and most dangerous recourse, is to swim out to the person in trouble.

Throughout the years, the National American Red Cross played the major role in training lifeguards. To obtain junior and then senior lifesaver certifications, a student passed rigorous physical tests, swimming long distances and treading water for prodigious periods of time. By demanding physical conditioning, the Red Cross hoped its lifeguards would have the strength and stamina to reach swimmers in need of rescue, and then use techniques to grab hold of and transport that panicked swimmer back to safety. Nonetheless, lifeguards succumbed with their victims, whose survival instincts were aimed at climbing up on, clawing and kicking the lifesaver.

An integral part of Red Cross lifesaving courses was instruction in what is now an obsolete procedure: artificial respiration. It was thought to be a mechanical method to bring air into the near-drowned victims' lungs and, coincidentally, encourage the regurgitation of ingested water. Lifeguards dragged victims up on the beach, arranged their unconscious bodies on their stomachs, cheek against the sand. The rescuer, stationed at the head, would then pull both elbows up and forward to expand the rib cage. These artificial expansions and contractions, it was hoped, would alternately pull in and expel air, reviving the drowning victim.

Rescue breathing was conceived in the 1950s as a way to keep bulbar polio victims, unable to breathe on their own, perfused with oxygen until they were placed in iron lungs, now known as respirators. More effective than artificial respiration, rescue breathing had the lifesaver exhaling the air in his lungs into the subject's mouth.

This worked for both the rescuer and victim because 80 percent of the oxygen we breathe is unused by our lungs and is exhaled. So if the lifesaver remembered to breathe normally and not hyperventilate, both he and his charge could breathe satisfactorily.

This procedure, an integral part of CPR, is still used for breathless patients—those not respiring but who still have a heartbeat. The continuing heart activity will keep the blood pumping through the body, distributing the oxygen being blown into the unconscious swimmer's mouth, and cells won't die.

Those who are breathless *and* pulseless (no heart activity) need rescue breathing plus some way to get their blood to circulate the oxygen. Artificial respiration has evolved into CPR. *Cardio*, for heart and *pulmonary* for lungs. Rescue breathing combines with chest compressions, which act like an artificial pump in lieu of the heart's beating. The oxygen is there; a pump is working. Both are provided by the person performing CPR.

Dive Rescue

Around the same time rescue breathing became an accepted medical procedure, underwater or dive rescue emerged. Dive rescue parallels the development of SCUBA and their commercial availability in the 1950s. PreSCUBA, divers wore huge, hard helmets or worked inside

---

Turtling Trucks

A frequently made mistake, common in books and screenplays, is to place a character in a submerged auto but still alive, breathing in a miraculous pocket of trapped air. While theoretically possible, this very rarely happens.

In real life, a vehicle will float for only forty to sixty seconds upon entering the water. Then, if it is in water deeper than it is long, it will turn turtle. Pulled by the weight of the engine, it will usually slowly cartwheel and end up on its roof. Any remaining air at this point usually bubbles out through chassis damage or is filled with floating debris.

An overturned car is very disorienting to both trapped victims and to the rescue divers. Furthermore, a current flow of only three mph exerts enough force to make it impossible to push open a closed door. The bottom line? Better forget about your character surviving an entrapment in sixteen feet of water.

---

a bell chamber. Both were tethered via ropes and air-supply hoses to boats and tenders on the surface, à la Jules Verne's *20,000 Leagues Under the Sea*. If a deep sea diver got in trouble, his lone hope was that his tenders would alert to tugs on the rope and pull him up.

In the mid-1950s, all of this changed.

Jacques Cousteau, SCUBA's inventor and chief publicist, told would-be divers they could discover the floor of the ocean free of their connections to the surface. Now their life-support systems could be worn on their backs. They could venture anywhere underwater as long as their air supply lasted. Consequently, a huge number of recreational divers discovered and explored the earth's underwater floor. And, of course, the popularity of SCUBA increased the need for underwater rescue.

More than any other rescue activity, dive rescue is driven by the clock. A submerged victim without air has a mere four to six minutes of survival time. Beyond that point, those bodily organs designated as vital—the heart, lungs, kidneys and brain—die without oxygen. This process cannot be reversed. The occasional exception to this rule is cold water drowning when lower water temperatures slow heartbeats and oxygen demands, prolonging sustainable life.

Dive rescue becomes appropriate in numerous scenarios: a car leaves the road and ends up in a lake, trapping your hero; a child playing on the edge of a sandpit falls in. But these rescues are time-driven.

As you work out the time factor in your story, be sure the call for help can go out with rescuer-response in four to six minutes or less if you wish your personality to survive intact. For this reason, most dive rescue is body-recovery work. The one exception is cold water near-drowning where the body functions might be decelerated to the point where cellular death is forestalled. (See chapter ten, "Winter Rescuer.")

Swiftwater Rescue

Like dive rescue, white or swiftwater river rescuers have carved out a new profession. In the past they weren't needed because canoeists and rafters quietly plied their sport in isolation. If they got into trouble, they knew there was no one else around to come to their aid; self-sufficiency was a part of the thrill. When John Powell's expedition ran a wild river, the geologist didn't know what was around the bend and had no way to pick his days and choose his rapids. He traveled blind, and understandably got into trouble. But early sporting canoeists and rafters could select their sites. They generally erred on the side of caution, culling out the dangerous slots, choosing their runs.

The recent surge of interest in kayaking accompanied by sweeping improvements in technology, materials and equipment opened the realms of river-running to everyone. Rapids judged too difficult to run just a few years ago are now easy for beginning paddlers. There are newly discovered and more treacherous river challenges ahead. There will also be a greater incidence of injuries and deaths. White-water boating is being pushed to its human and technological limits. Inevitably this means more business for white-water rescuers.

It is in the nature of wild rivers, those never dammed or controlled by man, that most of these rescues occur far from civilization. For that reason, professional river rescuers are the same people who work as the experienced practitioners and guides of the

These photographs show the Zumro dive-thru rescue boat in action. An inflatable boat designed for rescue, it has a "stack tube" construction permitting through-the-floor access for the rescuer or victim. The zippered-bow access hatch eliminates the problem of retrieving rescuers or victims from over the side of the boat. The boat holds a maximum of eight passengers, has an approximate speed of 25 to 30 mph, and is approximately seventeen feet long. (Photos © CMC Rescue, Inc., used by permission.)

Dead or Alive?

Near-drowning victims frequently are revived, only to succumb to death in the hospital. This is because their vital organs have suffered irreversible damage. The exception is the hypothermic individual whose state of partial freezing is not terribly different from the meat in your freezer. Just as bacterial activity slows in that leg of lamb or sausage, the human's bodily functions, including the dying of cells, become sluggish. This means that cold water drownings oftentimes can be revived even though the victims have been under water without oxygen for extended periods of time.

But when a normal-temperature human organism is deprived of oxygen for more than six minutes, irreversible cellular damage occurs. We cannot live long without well-running hearts, kidneys, lungs and brains. The key here is *long*. A person can still be alive with deadly damage to those vital organs, but only briefly. That's why so many drowning victims die two to three days after the event.

sport. They carry with them the tools of rescue and are in positions to accomplish the job.

While technological sophistication has improved gear, the process of wresting adults and children out of rushing water, whether in a flooding city street or recreational rapids, remains largely unchanged. Usually it is an exercise in time-honored technical rope maneuvers. The water rescuers' mantra of Reach/Throw/Row/Go is reduced to throwing ropes and flotation devices attached to lines. That is the most efficient means of rescue, and it also is safest for the rescuer.

Education and Certification

While water rescuers in the past were trained in artificial respiration, today's open and swiftwater rescue professionals are taught to render CPR. CPR is only performed on someone who is breathless and pulseless. A pulseless (no heartbeat) and breathless (no respirations) person is dead. The hope is to keep the victim's lifeless body in good enough shape for responding medical professionals to still be able to revive the victim. So it is important that the first rescuer knows CPR. It is a stopgap measure, a combination of pressured rescue breathing—air puffs from the rescuer's mouth into the victim's—

Rib Tickling

W riters tend to depict the chest compressions of CPR as a pressing down on the heart. In fact, those chest compressions are performed directly over the chest's midpoint, on the sternum or breastbone. As rescuers blow oxygen into the subject's mouth, the goal is to use the rib cage as a pumping mechanism, creating pressure on the entire chest cavity in order to shove that oxygen now in the lungs throughout the bloodstream. At the same time, the heart is pressured to empty out oxygenated blood, then refill with more of the same.

---

and then heart and chest cavity compression, which acts as a pump carrying oxygen through the lines to vital body parts. In literature, walking, talking people sometimes have CPR performed on them! Or people who are rigid, beyond ever being revived, are worked on. This is inaccurate writing.

Authors should take advantage of the fact that CPR can never be done wrong to the point where it injures because the person is already dead. When successful, all CPR does is keep the victim perfused, which means his blood is flowing and carrying oxygen. This is done until an EMT or medic comes along to defibrillate, or shock, the heart into a nice, normal beat. Medics also administer drugs to make the heart more responsive to that shock. When a book describes a miraculous coming-around after CPR, then the victim must not have been dead in the first place. And, incidentally, performing CPR on a live subject can be dangerous and even kill because the chest compressions might throw a beating heart into a disorganized, nonlife-sustaining rhythm called ventricular fibrillation. When subjects are in V-fib, they are dead.

Lifeguards, and in fact all professional rescuers, have a special professional rescuer CPR-certification under the auspices of the Red Cross or American Heart Association. (AHA no longer calls it certification, to limit their exposure. They only admit to the training, not the competence of the CPR student.) The professional rescuer training, in comparison to civilian CPR, includes two-person CPR: one rescuer does the rescue breathing, the second rescuer compresses the chest.

In addition to CPR courses, swiftwater rescue courses are available to backcountry guides and riverside community emergency management teams. This education relies on rope and belaying techniques, and stresses familiarity with the latest equipment.

Because helicopter (helo) maneuvers might be utilized when the victim's location is otherwise impossible to reach, your character will have helo training. In actuality, helo rescue has been known to be executed inappropriately. Overenthusiastic responders suffering from rescue syndrome like to call out the chopper when it is not needed or is not the most efficient means of transport. Many deaths can be attributed to nonemergency helo missions. They make great stories.

Internal crew training is necessary for a helo team to work. This team will collectively know to never place their own lives at risk for a body recovery, a DOA. Your rescuer will be knowledgeable about lowering and lifting tactics while the helicopter hovers over water. He'll be familiar with ground chopper procedures and hot landing strategies—when there is only enough clear space or decent weather to touch down and take off fast.

When a hot landing is impossible, there is an even more dangerous alternative: short hauling, which is exactly what it sounds like— a person is clipped into and dangled from a rope or cable, then flown to the critical area. If you want to include it in your rescue, make sure it is a last resort. Helo rescue using a short haul is not a carnival act; it is serious, deadly and overused. You can accurately have a disaster result from your short haul.

Water safety instructor certification is a common competence-level for water rescue crews. More highly specialized rescuers will have been trained as rescue swimmers, passing challenging endurance tests. These are the folks who will jump out of helicopters or boats into raging floodwaters and storm-tossed seas. Many are graduates of the U.S. Navy's SEAL program.

Job Description

When a diver wearing SCUBA gear is entrapped, the hope would be that his diving buddy was certified and knowledgeable in water rescue. Given the four-to-six-minute window of opportunity to prevent irreversible kidney, brain and heart damage, the rescuer needs to already be in the water with the victim or it is too late.

Only when there appears to be a body recovery, or when the subject stands a good chance of being trapped in a pocket of air (doubtful in a submerged vehicle; possible in a cave) would it make sense for your frantic characters to activate from a distant point a SCUBA rescue team.

As part of their training, divers are taught ways to share their air with others who, while submerged, have either run out of air or have mechanical malfunction with, or damage to, their SCUBA equipment. If both players remain calm, the technique for shared air is little more than exchanging the mouthpiece of functioning equipment, like passing a peace pipe back and forth. If the breathless diver is (understandably) panicked, then the situation is hazardous to the rescuer. He must not approach unless he is certain he can control the other diver. The danger is that the rescuer's air supply will be seized by the other, and the rescuer will involuntarily switch positions with the victim.

Another common rescue diving risk is what the medical community calls barotrauma and the dive community calls decompression sickness or, more commonly, the bends. All body tissues contain some dissolved gasses, nitrogen and oxygen in particular. Too much dissolved nitrogen is a killer. Its presence in the bloodstream increases as the diver multiplies pressure on his body by diving. For every thirty-three feet of depth, the amount of pressure doubles and so does the amount of dissolved nitrogen.

If the body doesn't have time to compensate for and eliminate these dissolved gasses as it rises through the water (through ever-diminishing pressures until one atmosphere or surface-level pressure is reached), nitrogen bubbles out of the blood and causes trouble in the body tissues. The bubbles like to take up residence in the joints, causing such extreme pain that it makes the sufferer hunch over in anguish. The bends.

Along with joint-problems, these nitrogen bubbles travel throughout the system causing headaches, nausea, paralysis and death. Sometimes barotrauma is immediately apparent after a rapid rise and decompression; other times its symptoms wait twelve to thirty hours before presenting themselves.

The best way to treat decompression sickness is to repressurize the subject. The patient is sealed inside a hyperbaric or dive chamber and, over hours, the atmospheric pressure is gradually increased until the amount experienced during the dive is reached. This higher pressure will drive the nitrogen bubbles back into solution. Finally, the patient is decompressed, allowing excess gasses to be naturally expired.

Because this medical process of atmospheric compression and decompression, called diving, takes time, hyperbaric chambers are large enough so that professionals can monitor the patient during the many hours it takes.

If your character is a dive rescuer, she would know not to ascend too rapidly either by herself or with a victim. But barotrauma still happens, whether driven by necessity or by accident. In either case, victims will be transported to the nearest dive chamber, which can be hundreds of miles away, and undergo long hours of compression and decompression. Incidentally, if your heroine is well trained, she will know not to take a plane ride to the nearest hyperbaric chamber because the altitude and pressure changes in flight will only compound the trauma.

Rescue swimmers might be in a position to rescue a surfaced diver with the bends. Rescue swimmers are powerful and hardy, capable of supporting themselves and another in the water. These athletes are knowledgeable small boat handlers and, if swiftwater rescuers, are expert kayakers, canoeists and rafters.

Kayaks, canoes and rafts have a place in white-water emergencies. Trained water rescuers will size up the situation by reading the river and understanding where the victim is or will surface, will analyze available resources and their locations, and then plan how to employ them. All of this must happen quickly.

Then the Reach/Throw/Row/Go concept, mentioned earlier in the chapter, comes into play.

• Reach: The first step in a rescue for a paddler adrift is to try and reach her with an arm-extender like a branch. Is the pull of the white water too far to reach from shore? Then something must be thrown.

- Throw: A white-water rescuer has a nifty resource: rope laid in a football-sized, nylon stuff sack. The line inside this loosely stuffed throw bag is made of polypropylene because its plastic weave will float on the surface. It is yellow for visibility. A weighted end can be thrown up to about sixty feet, directly to or over the boater or swimmer. The victim can latch onto it and either be pulled to safety or swing with the current towards the shore downstream from the thrower, where another rescuer will be waiting. Because the length of rope is fixed, the thrower must position herself the correct distance from the site of rescue. River rescue ropes, either single- or double-coiled, would also be tried, depending on conditions and the position of the person needing rescue. These ropes have the advantage of being controllable in terms of the length thrown. If none of this works, it is time to consider getting in a boat to reach the subject.

- Row: If the paddler is trapped in the river, pinned by the current, snagged by a fallen tree or wedged into a crack, there may be no choice but to row to him while wearing an umbilical rope tied to the shore. If this isn't possible, the rescuers must consider swimming out or being lowered to make the rescue.

- Go: To accomplish this step, rescuers are connected to one another as well as to the shore. If all is failure and disaster, at least they can make their way back to dry land.

Other enhancements on Reach/Throw/Row/Go might include rigging fixed and movable ropes across the river, using the current to position rescuers and increasing what is called their mechanical advantage. Pulley systems like Z-drags are the most common. A Z-drag arranges ropes and carabiners to pull more weight than one could by directly tugging on a straight line. Thus every pound of pull can move two pounds or more of weight.

When the distressed passengers are on board something larger than a kayak or raft, Coast Guard personnel get involved. They use choppers to deliver rescuers by cable and winch. These dropped USCG swimmers round up victims in the water and, one-by-one,

---

Cooling Your Character's Heels

A person stands a good chance of surviving immersion in 50° water for fifteen minutes and will lose consciousness in sixty minutes. In 33° water, the victim will sustain herself for no more than five minutes and will be unconscious in less than fifteen minutes.

---

get them into horse collars or baskets to be hauled to safety by the hovering helicopter.

If those in need of help are on board a failing ship, rescuers might be lowered from the helicopter or transferred from ships to organize the rescue. This rescue operation might involve installing and manning large pumps to keep damaged boats and equipment afloat until the storm passes or the ship can be safely brought to port.

If seas are stormy and the Coast Guard cutter cannot tie up next to the endangered ship, lifeboats will move between the boats. As a last recourse, breeches buoys will be strung from ship to ship and victims transferred the old way. No matter the method chosen, the transfer to and from the rescue scene is the most perilous part of the job.

Frequently during water rescue operations, rescue personnel encounter a person chilled by cold ocean or lake waters. Water temperatures, colder than body temperatures, conduct body heat away at twice the rate of air. These cold-challenged individuals will act goofy or sleepy and lethargic, as if they are intoxicated.

Medical rescuers have a number of techniques to *slowly* rewarm these characters, including administering 98.6° IVs and heated blankets. Patients might also be swaddled in body heat-reflective materials. The first step though, as all rescuers know, is to get the victim out of the cold water and air, cut away the wet clothing and dry the body to limit heat loss due to evaporation.

Unlike swift and deep water rescuers, dive rescue specialists are called out for particular missions but otherwise spend their time doing something else. In contrast, lifeguards are on the scene, watching and waiting. Images of the TV program *Baywatch* to the contrary, the job of a lifeguard can be boring—long hours spent in the hot sun doing not much more than scanning crowds of swimmers and acres of beach. Still, a lifeguard must always be ready to spring into action, knowing that she has only a few minutes to effect a rescue.

Increasingly, lifeguard downtime is spent in preventive activities. Guards train children and adults to be stronger swimmers, better able to take care of themselves in the water and more aware of their capabilities. Competitions, both inter- and intra-beach, are often the medium of choice for this conditioning.

The other common preventive guard activity is to walk and study the beach, following the changing weather and surf patterns. Lifeguards will know where and when tidal rips develop and what sections of the beach may have an undertow. They will be able to judge both present and developing surf patterns to know when and where it will be safe for the public to swim. Unsafe areas and conditions will be closed to swimming.

The lifesaving part of a lifeguard's job is two-part. The first step is to use whatever technique is safest to pull the drowning person from the water. Then, once ashore, the guard will initiate CPR without delay on any pulseless, nonbreathing person while she awaits the arrival of EMS. Because CPR is only done on dead people and, done right, it is not a pretty sight, it is easy to imagine a scene on the beach where the lifeguard labors heroically to revive the drowned person while a crowd of curious bystanders looks on. Almost invariably during this episode, the victim will throw up several pints of inhaled water and then copious amounts of his last meal. Messy. Very messy. It's not usually written about this way.

Equipment

For open or deep water rescue, the important tools are her flotation device and her suit. The high-visibility flotation gear is heavy-duty and securely fastened. These special rescue vests are made so one rescuer can clip onto another. No matter its style or design, it will support the rescue swimmer floating on her back, head out of water. Secured to its front, within easy reach, will be a whistle and flares, emergency locating beacons and a rescue knife in addition to one strapped to her belt or thigh. The rescuer will also carry, float or throw such vests out to the victims.

The suit a swimmer wears may be one of three distinct types. Wet suits, made of soft neoprene rubber, are formfitting, gussetted at the ankle and zippered down the front, allowing the swimmer to easily move and work in the water. These suits allow a thin layer of water to accumulate between the swimmer's skin and suit. As soon as this water warms to body temperature, it acts as further insulation and protection from the cold. Gloves, booties, hoods, fins, face masks and snorkels are added.

In contrast, a dry suit is just that. Designed to keep out all water, its various seals are tighter and more complicated. They, too, incorporate fins, booties, mittens and hoods for extra protection and maneuverability.

The final choice for rescue swimmers in extreme environments is a suit substituting greater insulation and cold protection for ease of motion. Some of these suits can even be inflated from SCUBA tanks, leaving the wearer looking something like a Gumby—and a warm one at that. These rescue suits are more cumbersome than either wet or dry suits.

This swiftwater rescuer wears a neoprene wetsuit during a rescue. The red color of the suit increases the rescuer's visibility. Some wetsuits are now made of titanium. (Photo used by permission of Harvey Eisner.)

The well-equipped water rescuer will have an all-weather storm whistle that produces a high-frequency sound easily heard over the noise of wind and waves. The whistle does not have a "pea" that will stick or swell, so it even works under water. (Photo © CMC Rescue, Inc., used by permission.)

No matter what outfit, divers wear weights in their vests, around their waists, or in backpacks to enable them to stay below the water's surface.

The only remaining piece of gear a deep water rescuer needs is a way to get out of the water. This may be a small boat or life raft that she can scramble into. Alternatively, she may need to be lowered from and hoisted back up into a helicopter. In the latter case, she may have a harness built into her life jacket so she can clip in for the raising or lowering. Or she may use a horse collar, which is a U-shaped piece of flotation, that can support two people while they are being pulled up. Finally, there are different plastic or metal baskets that hold several people and can be raised or lowered.

For divers wearing wet or dry suits, there are a variety of underwater lights that can be carried and worn. In dark or turbid conditions, dive rescuers will swim with a tag line, which is a tether to the shore and to a tender who looks after them should they ever get into trouble. In searches, as this same tag line gets played out, it helps to keep track of areas surveyed.

Dive rescuers will wear an underwater watch to keep track of the time of the dive and the amount of air left in his tanks. These same instruments may have built-in depth gauges. It is essential for the dive rescuer to always know how long it will take him to ascend to normal pressures and to be certain that he has enough air left to accomplish this safely.

Lifeguards don't worry about suits and protection from the cold. If the weather and the water aren't warm enough, people won't be swimming and the beaches will be closed. But they do need whistles and bullhorns to warn swimmers away from danger. In addition, they are equipped with rescue ropes, flotation devices and a surfboard or shorter flotation board to transport them quickly to a swimmer in distress and provide buoyancy for the two of them.

On the larger beaches in year-round warm climates (southern California is a good example), lifeguards will be in touch with one another and their control via portable radios. They may have on call any number of boats and vehicles to transport themselves, their gear and their victims.

White-water rescuers wear wet or dry suits, sometimes abbreviated to cover just the torso if the air and water temperatures are tolerable. They wear flotation devices or safety vests to keep them afloat if they get into trouble. They also wear helmets, which will protect them should they be swept out of control downriver.

Their equipment is sized to fit on their boats: throw bags containing rope and coils of rope, a variety of carabiners and maybe some mechanical devices (brakes, pulleys and prusiks) borrowed from the world of technical rescue, extra clothing and wraps for warmth. These plus ingenuity are about all the river rescuer can bring to his place of work.

In more populated areas where river rescue is common, such as Pittsburgh with its confluence of three rivers or the island of Manhattan, swiftwater rescuers use powered boats and fire access gear such as extension ladders. Line guns are used to transfer rope across a raging river. They shoot a thin haul line tied to a larger rescue rope. This would be the first step in a Tyrolean rescue, which is a stretched rope-and-pulley maneuver.

Language

BOIL LINE The point where circulating water bubbles to the surface in a hole.

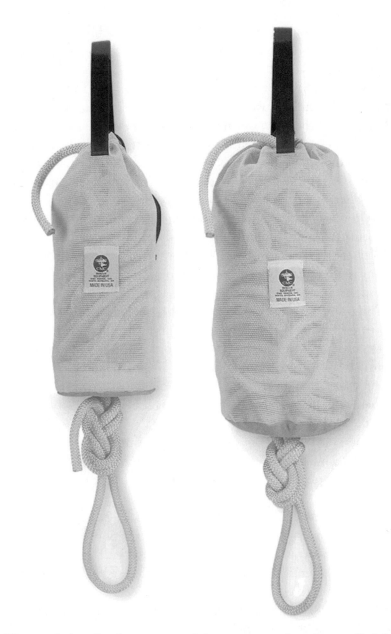

These mesh throwline bags are part of the water rescuer's equipment. Both bags feature a quick-release strap and top handle and hold $^7/_{16}$-inch rope. The smaller bag holds a thirty-five foot throwline, the larger one a seventy-five foot throwline. (Photo © CMC Rescue, Inc., used by permission.)

BROACHING The sideways turning of a boat due to the current.

BUOYANCY CONTROL DEVICE (BCD) Used to bring up a fallen diver, it counteracts the diver's weight system. BCDs are also excellent as swimming aids for exhausted victims.

COLD WATER NEAR-DROWNING In cold water, due to MDR, the chances of survival are improved. The colder the water, the better the chance. A common axiom of emergency medicine is: A cold water near-drowning is not dead until warm and dead.

CUSHION A pillow of water piling up around an object in a river, like a bridge pier or stone.

DROWNING A death caused by submersion in the water. A victim is suffocated by water intake through the mouth and into the lungs. Eight thousand people die annually due to drowning. Of these, 40 percent are under five years of age.

DRY DROWNING The first gulp of cold water causes the larynx to spasm shut. As the throat closes, the victim is suffocated and the lungs stay empty.

EDDIES Pockets of calm water often moving in a circle or upstream, located on the downstream side of obstructions, like rocks.

ENTRAPMENT Snagged by the force of the water.

HAYSTACKS Standing waves that mark the deepest and fastest pitches.

HOLE A reverse current that tends to trap and hold a buoyant object; also called a pourover, vertical eddy, stopper, reversal or sousehole.

HYDRAULIC Water pressure as in a hole.

MAMMALIAN DIVING REFLEX (MDR) Whenever the face is suddenly submerged in cold water, cardiac output and the heartbeat are reduced so that although the blood flow continues to the brain, it is restricted elsewhere in the body. Other diving mammals have the same slowdown response with sufficient blood to their brain cells, which keeps them alive for long periods underwater. Heat is preserved when blood flow is restricted to the body core and not to the limbs.

PENDULUMING One end of a rescue rope is belayed upstream while the other is held by a swimmer who can surf the downstream current to the same shore.

PIN What happens to a boat when held against a hard object by the water's force.

RAPIDS An area of rough turbulent water flow.

RIFFLES Small waves, often symmetrical in appearance, caused by swift current and shallows.

RIVER A rapidly flowing body of water moving through a channel characterized by numerous rapids, waterfalls and obstacles.

STRAINERS A submerged object, like a tree with water running under and over it, that combs the water. Strainers block the passage of objects in the current, such as a swimmer or a boat.

WET DROWNING Water fills the lungs; 75 to 80 percent of all drownings are wet drownings.

WHITE WATER Any stream, creek, waterfall, river or other rapidly flowing body of water that creates turbulence as it flows over, around and through natural or human-made obstacles.

Dangers

From cliff to surf-washed shoreline, from overflowing river to rock-bound canyon, from quiet lake to drainage-filled culvert, water can be an insidious, overpowering foe. An experienced water rescuer respects the power of water and its hidden dangers.

Often, though, it is not the water that gets the rescuer but the victim being rescued. Fear of drowning is galvanizing; the victim can discover superhuman powers to try to save himself. The world of water rescue is full of stories of rescuers being overwhelmed by panicked victims, of mouthpieces ripped out and air tanks pulled off backs, of frantic people climbing up on the shoulders of their saviors in an attempt to get out of and above the water.

Victims can be dangerous; so can the weather. Ocean and river waters in particular tend to be cold. Depending upon the season, they can be just above freezing or they can be in the fifties and low sixties. For river scenarios, remember that the best river running is in the spring when the rivers are full of snowmelt and cold spring rains.

Along with cold, swiftwater rescuers deal with the force of the rushing river water. Even while they are rushing to accomplish a rescue, river rescuers have to be sure to not get swept downstream,

Stabilizing the victim is crucial to a successful water rescue. This rescuer, wearing full scuba gear, has strapped the victim to a floating stretcher. The firefighters then pulled the victim to land. (Photo courtesy of Ferno-Washington.)

becoming entrapped by the force of the water against a rock or log, snared by a crack or jam, or otherwise maimed or killed. This type of accident is not uncommon.

Ocean rescuers, particularly in warm waters, cannot afford to forget they are not alone. Portuguese men-of-war, stingrays, stonefish, lionfish and cone shells are but a few of the stinging population of the seas. Then there are sharks and barracuda. One eye always has to be peeled for the unexpected.

Given the profile of the victim in distress, water rescue is inherently risky. Eighty-five percent of near-drowning victims are male and two-thirds do not know how to swim. A significant portion of male drownings are found with high blood-alcohol levels, and with their flies unzipped. Why? Intoxicated fishermen or male boaters relieve themselves over the gunwales or into the water from shore, and accidentally fall in.

CHAPTER NINE

Rope Rescuer

R ope is a tool. It has been around for thousands of years, whether in the form of braided leather, horsehair, natural fiber or some form of high-tech nylon. It allows rescuers to climb up and down otherwise impassable walls; it reaches across perilous environments; it pulls up weights and, with the addition of simple tools, it increases the mechanical advantage of any lifting system. From the point of view of rescue, it can safely move rescuers on-scene and it can be used to retrieve both rescuers and victims.

In this day of technical climbing, a sport where gear is essential and seems to be ever changing, it is important to remember that rope is little more than a tool needed to accomplish specific chores. The popularity of technical or rock climbing is increasing the need for rope rescue, but not as much as might be imagined. Rock climbers are still proving themselves to be an independent group; nine times out of ten they will self-rescue. Rope rescue, however, is an integral part of swiftwater rescues; fire, cave and confined space rescues; and attempted suicide rescues.

History of the Profession

Until World War II, ropes were made of natural fibers such as hemp, sisal or cotton, and twisted together to make strands. These strands in turn were twisted tightly together to create the rope. This is the laid construction technique.

Alpinists carried such natural-fiber ropes. At sea, manila ropes were the sinews that held together the masts and sails of the great ships, handy when thrown with a life ring to rescue a man overboard.

But the rescue applications of these laid ropes were limited. They were heavy and did not last long under exposure to the elements and to abrasion. They stretched under light (body weight) loads, but had no give under high-impact loads. They were rough to work with and tended to unwind under a hanging or free load. Your character will find that they kink and don't easily feed through pulleys.

Under the impetus of World War II, nylon ropes came into play. Developed for marine uses, these goldline ropes (a trade name that has become a generic) were stronger and resisted rot. They also stretched under a heavy load, which meant they didn't transmit a sudden impact to a falling climber. If a free-falling body is stopped by a manila rope, the stop is a sudden shock, capable of breaking a back. With nylon rope, the impact is gradual, even gentle as the rope stretches as it is loaded.

These new ropes came to be considered dynamic ropes because of their give. They cushioned the end of a free fall, then recovered their original strength and condition. Dynamic ropes, in contrast to the older or static ropes, made possible the sport of rock climbing and accelerated the development of the rope rescue profession.

Over the years, nylon ropes have continued to improve, ending up as today's cutting-edge rope, the kernmantle. Since the 1970s, these dynamic ropes have been manufactured with a core of continuous fibers surrounded by a tightly braided nylon sheath. They have abrasion resistance, high strength, low-impact force and low stretch under body weight.

Kernmantle rope is an excellent rescue tool. Light enough for your slight female rescuer to haul, it is easily thrown or shot distances. It feeds through pulleys, rollers, brakes and carabiners, and withstands rough usage in difficult settings. Finally, it will hold the weight of your woman, plus the 200-pound man she is rescuing. Should she lose her footing during the rescue, it will gently stop their fall.

The history of rope rescue is the history of rope. As it improved, high-angle rescuers utilized it in more imaginative and resourceful ways. Simultaneously, the sport of rock climbing brought about an array of tools and fastenings that made hitherto unthinkable climbs possible. The rope rescue profession has been borrowing and adapting these same tools to its peculiar needs in a variety of contexts far from rock pitches, cliffs and boulders.

All rescue professionals are familiar with rope rescue techniques. And every rescue vehicle carries a couple of coils of different-weight ropes. When the going gets bad in a rope rescue and there is a professional rope rescuer available, one will be called, whether the rescue is a collapsed trench, motor vehicle accident, hazmat incident or fire. Rope rescuers will lower a stricken crane operator, cross a flooded river to rescue a farm family trapped on the roof of their home, evacuate a climber who fell fifty feet down a steep granite slab, and extricate a caver who broke her leg two hundred feet below the Earth's surface.

Education and Certification

Professional rope rescuers are themselves recreational climbers. Climbing is a hugely popular sport; with all of the climbers out there, any rescue team near the mountains will have a specialist in rope rescue. In mountainous areas, advanced recreational climbers have banded together to form their own, often highly professional rope rescue teams. They can be turned out with a 911 phone call, ready to leave jobs for the next adventure. Many such team members wear pagers for this purpose, or a team might have a telephone tree. They stay active with the group, continuously training together

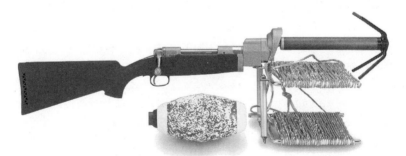

The Tetra line thrower shoots ropes up to ¹/₂-inch in thickness over all types of terrain. The mounted grappling hook is used for mountain and urban rescues while the float can be mounted for water rescue. Using .308 caliber blanks for propulsion, the line thrower can be quickly loaded and fired under severe conditions, even while wearing gloves. (Photo © CMC Rescue, Inc., used by permission.)

because they know they could be the next victim in need of rope rescue.

Ranger units have men and women with these particular skills. In all cases, the rope rescue specialist will first be an expert climber, then will add rescue training to his skills.

In the cities, rope rescue is handled through fire departments, which will have a team of specialists skilled in raising and lowering.

It may be difficult to tell whether an interest in climbing led to an interest in rope rescue or the reverse. In any case, the two go hand in hand as they use the same skills and materials. They also demand a certain attitude and confidence, a sense that the impossible can be made both possible and safe.

Fire departments and rescue squads conduct their own classroom and practical training sessions in vertical rope rescue. These are the best ways for a team to develop the tight relationship that enables rescuers to work well together. Individuals must learn to trust their partners so that in difficult situations, everyone can focus on the job at hand. Hanging from a rope seventy-five feet above a river is not the time to wonder if your buddy remembered to back the bowline knot that ties you into your harness.

There are high-angle rope rescue programs throughout the country offering skills training with as many as four different levels of rope rescue expertise. Graduates of these programs become the in-service trainers in their home services. In this way, word, skills and innovations spread.

The most important thing that any rope rescuer knows is that the rope, rigged and belayed properly, will stop his fall. This knowledge is what gives him the confidence to reach that extra two or three inches during a rescue operation. To drive home this point, prospective rescuers will be pushed to precarious positions on cliffs and training walls and then asked to strip off or shove away from the wall and free fall. Peeling or pushing off from a near-vertical surface is an important part of climbing experience because climbers are going down as far away from the surface as possible. The alternative on the way down is to risk banging into knobs and wedging into cracks.

Free Falls

All too often the media tends to create characters who walk away from tumbles. Rope rescuers are acutely aware of the dangers of a free fall. They know that a good rule of thumb, supported by EMS data, is that any plunge twice as long as the victim is tall can result in serious trauma. So when a three-foot-high toddler loses his grip on a six-foot-high jungle gym, the possibility of serious harm is present. This should put the dangers that a rope rescuer faces into perspective. Rescues off sheer cliffs and down rock faces do not leave room for mistakes.

As his anchors and belays hold him on his first and subsequent training falls, the novice rescuer survives and comes to trust his equipment and rigging. He learns that the rope dynamically slows and stops the fall. This exercise develops the confidence to push the limits of technique and to learn to trust the rope systems so that attention can remain focused on the rescue.

The Mountain Rescue Association and NASAR cosponsor the annual North American Technical Rescue Symposium. Peers share news and views on advances in equipment, technical problems and professional issues.

Qualifications

Rope rescuers have well-developed arms and upper bodies, but are also nimble and flexible. They have good hands and the ability to make precise finger and wrist movements. It is not unusual to see climbers squeezing a tennis ball or round rubber doughnut during their free time to condition and strengthen their hands and forearms. The next time they are on the rope, they may be able to accomplish just a little bit more, to hang a little bit longer while their feet grope for a tiny bit of support.

Rope rescuers *know* rope, along with knots, harnesses and hardware. Mentally and physically steady, rational and ordered, they size up a situation and then rig the response to meet the need. Because every situation is different, they are inventive.

Along with tennis balls, a rope rescuer might be seen playing with lengths of rope. He can tie knots blindfolded. He has complete

---

No Pain, No Pain

Any good technical climber—and these are the folks who get into rescue—continues to enjoy the sport because there is more pleasure than pain, more highs than lows, and lows in technical climbing get serious. The only way to reap the joys is to combine the laws of physics with the art of accomplishing the seemingly impossible. If one does not do this, the pain overtakes the pleasure as the body takes unnecessary punishment. These people would have dropped out of the sport long before they were at the rescuer level.

---

confidence in the bulletproof knots he ties to create his rigging. His life, along with the life of a victim and partner, depend upon it.

Rope rescuers, who have good survival instincts, also have an intuitive sense of physics. Much of what they do is predicated upon mechanical advantage. They will need to rig systems that increase the lift or pull of a line so that a single person can move objects five and six times heavier than his own weight. They will also need to tension a horizontal line to reduce the sag when it is weighted in the middle.

There is no such thing as a careless climber who has been at the sport for the long haul. This is a sport that swiftly and decisively punishes carelessness. The primary source of concern for rescuers and climbers alike is the integrity of their ropes. Each rope is labeled and its purchase date recorded. They are examined for rips or tears. These rescuers keep track of how many falls and from what height each of their ropes has stopped. Ropes get retired for safety reasons when they still look fine.

No one steps on the ropes. Rescuers go ballistic at the risk of sheath-abrasion caused by such thoughtlessness. And when the ropes are stowed, they are pushed, not coiled, into stuff sacks or laundry-baglike rope bags, out of the reach of harmful ultraviolet rays or accidentally spilled chemicals.

There is a climbing tradition to work clean and lean. The environment should be left as it was found; nothing should be disturbed. Rock climbers try to remove all signs of the aids and protection they may have placed on the way up. Rope rescue is a different animal. When on a rescue, these folks, while they may be climbing purists,

---

Towering Rescue

Tower crane rescue, a new specialty, is a close relative of rope rescue. According to expert rescuer Tom Vines in his *Rescue Report*, the more challenging efforts have involved crane operators who have been electrocuted when contacting exposed wiring or experienced medical emergencies such as heart attacks. The rescue is then twofold: The subject must be raised out of the crane's tight operator cab, and then lowered. Training in and with cranes is necessary to understand the problems and solutions.

---

are interested in safety combined with speed. They place their screws into rock, use whatever extra rope makes sense, cut branches and move soil. This is not sport; it is saving lives.

Job Description

Individuals hired by national and state parks as rangers might be professional rope rescuers. Generally, those whose expertise includes rope rescue are a part of a team with other specialists. Both paid and unpaid professional SAR teams in wilderness response areas include rope rescuers. There are people who respond when needed but are not sitting, awaiting a call. Rope rescuers either have other related responsibilities or work at other positions and are available when a victim is in distress.

Equipment

In addition to rope and webbing, this rescuer carries water for himself and his potential victim, along with minimal medical supplies. If he is a medical provider as well, he'll carry a stethoscope and IV equipment. If your rope rescuer will be climbing or rappelling to reach the victim, he will wear a backpack. If the weather is not harsh, he will dress lightly in spandex materials, perhaps in a sleeveless muscle shirt. If he needs to climb a rock face, his shoes will look like laced-up ballet shoes, soft and pliable. Otherwise, he will be wearing climbing boots. He may wear a bandana to catch perspiration so his sight is not obscured.

The responder who must effect a technical rescue, whether along a sheer wall or from a skyscraper, wears a climbing harness with

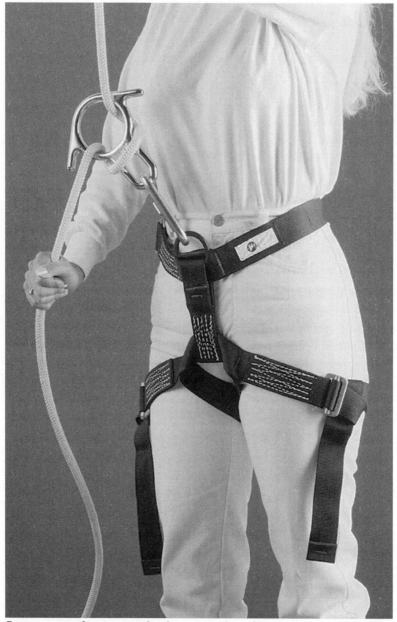

Rope rescuers often use a utility harness, such as this one made by CMC Rescue. The metal ring at the top of the harness is called a D-ring and is proof rated at five thousand pounds. Note also the figure 8 belaying device, clipped into the D-ring. (Photo © CMC Rescue, Inc., used by permission.)

straps around his waist and hips and between his legs. This is in lieu of a seat and is a support to clip onto. This distributes the load and frees his hands, allowing him to move a subject in a special patient harness with him. This diaper-like cradling device attaches with three divisions to a single point. The rescuer's waist strap clangs with the hardware of climbing.

Pulleys, hitches and even cranes are available to the rescuer when it is necessary to lower a subject.

The difference in the equipment of a sport technical climber and a rope rescuer is weight. Unlike the technical climber, who will often hike distances to reach his chosen site, the rescuer will not be carrying his equipment for miles, so it does not have to be lightweight.

Language

AID A device used by a climber to help him get up a rock.

ALPINISM Sport combining rock and ice climbing, cross-country skiing and hiking to reach the summit of a mountain.

ANCHOR A solid point to which a rescuer can tie himself or a rope.

ASCENDER A mechanical device to help climb up a rope.

BELAY Anchoring one end of a rope by either tying it off or using friction to control it dynamically; a method to gradually stop a fall.

This rope rescue kit contains the equipment necessary to set up a raising, lowering, or belay system for over-the-side rescue. It includes anchor and release straps, a pulley, D carabiners, a personal carabiner, an anchor plate, ascenders, and several types of cords. Rope rescuers, perhaps more than any other type of rescuer, are fanatics about the state of their equipment. (Photo © CMC Rescue, Inc., used by permission.)

CARABINER An indispensable small, oval aluminum or steel loop with a locking, swinging gatelike opening, used to clip together everything one can imagine while climbing. Rope rescuers carry a dozen different-size carabiners on their harness's belt.

DESCENDER A mechanical device to help the rescuer go down a rope.

DYNAMIC The use of friction generated by wrapping a rope around the waist or a tree or using a mechanical brake device to control weight on a rope.

LEAD First member of the rescue party up.

RAPPEL A controlled descent down a rope.

TYROLIAN TRAVERSE Lateral belay-and-transfer system used to transport rescuers and subjects across canyons and rivers; a rope bridge.

Dangers

The dangers a rope rescuer faces are real. The maneuvers he accomplishes are difficult when working alone; as he transports a victim, they are treacherous.

There's an old line about rope rescue. The danger's not in the fall, but in the landing. In addition to that splat hazard, these rescuers suffer from mashed fingers and toes. They hurt their backs and get hit with falling rocks and boulders. They are susceptible to hyperthermia in summer and hypothermia in winter.

As rescue responders cut themselves, they patch their wounds with instant glue. There have been problems when this improvement on Band-aids was not completely dried as the rope rescuer continued his climb.

Bruises and blisters are an occupational hazard. Duct tape, sometimes referred to as gray medical tape, is applied to such abrasions. It is protective and smooth enough so the rescue climb can continue.

A commonly made error in rescue writing is to have a character tied to a rope as he wades or swims out on a rescue. This is wrong! Have your rescuer carry the end of the rope in his hand or wear a quick-release harness. Otherwise, there is too much chance of the rope getting snagged and your hero being trapped. On the other hand, if you wish to kill off someone, here's your mechanism.

Winter Rescuer

B ecause of the weather, winter is when simply getting lost turns into a matter of life or death. Unless, of course, the victim is rescued.

The demands this form of rescue places on the responder make this professional as durable and impressive as the life-sustaining gear. Wintertime makes every step of the rescue process, tough in less harsh climates or on city streets, harshly difficult.

Winter rescuers are versatile. They might be winter guides who earn their living in the wilderness, as rangers or as volunteer rescue team members with other full-time professions. They are prepared to deal with avalanches moving at eighty miles per hour and packing enough force to pulverize concrete; with thin ice stretched over freezing cold water; with sheer ice-coated cliffs and waterfalls; and with snowstorms so fierce they can't see their hands before their eyes. They have spent lifetimes on frosty mountains and austere crags, usually all over the world. They love a challenge, or what they would categorize as a peak experience.

Rescue is the greatest high of all; a human life is at stake. The most accomplished alpinists, ice climbers, extreme skiers, rock climbers and polar explorers are pushed to their limits when they go out to save someone who, more often than not, is seriously traumatized, medically hypothermic, frightened and operating with an altered sensorium. It's dealing with a crazy person on the edge of the planet with nowhere to go but down.

It's a neat way to test the mettle of a man or woman. Winter rescuers won't usually talk about this, although it is a significant part of the impetus.

Skyblazer dye marker is used by winter rescuers to signal other rescuers or to mark trails. The orange powder turns snow or water bright fluorescent green on contact. (Photo © CMC Rescue, Inc., used by permission.)

History of the Profession

Winter rescue as a calling is an amalgam of rope and water rescue techniques stressed and pushed within the context of a severe environment. To those skills are added the experiences of ski patrollers, ice climbers, searchers and winter sport enthusiasts.

Aside from Donner Party sagas and Peruvian airplane crashes like the one described in the best-seller, *Alive!*, the thing that got winter rescue going was the Arctic and Antarctic expeditions of Byrd, Amundsen, Peary and Nansen. Those folks demonstrated that a frigid climate that people tried to avoid at all costs could be survivable and, indeed, fascinating.

Added to the mix are trappers and loggers who have spent winters outdoors for centuries. They, too, evolved clothing and lifestyles that made even the most extreme cold survivable.

Along with the polar explorers, loggers and trappers, the post-Victorian rusticators headed for the wilderness in all seasons. In the early twentieth century, as Adirondack furniture was being fashioned from branches, Indians and Eskimos became fashionable and Teddy Roosevelt led the nation in big game hunting. The out-of-doors grew into the newest playground for the affluent.

Winter sports continue to be an expensive game, with equipment and garb field-tested on expeditions to the far corners of the world. Manufacturers of extreme sports-outfitters base their advertising campaigns on these comprehensive trials.

Gear- and clothing-intensive, the costs of winter rescue would be ruinous to the average American. One must be committed to the play, or to the rescue, or both. Winter rescuers who travel to those in distress come from a mix of those who work in the environment and those who are recreational winter enthusiasts—high-altitude climbers, downhill skiers, backcountry adventurers—who already own the winter-survival gear.

Because the environment is so tough, anybody calling herself a winter rescuer will be physically comfortable in the harsh climate with a variety of rescue techniques. This is necessary because in a split second, one type of disaster can turn into another. A ranger might be snowshoeing in search of a hunter, a known diabetic, who is two days' overdue. She may track that wanderer to a stream at the top of a waterfall. Looking over the fall, she might spot the arm of a blaze-orange jacket 150 feet below. In order to complete the rescue, she is going to have to access the subject by descending the ice wall.

Education and Certification

Because of the conditions, potential responders are required by a team or organization to demonstrate their ability to navigate in winter conditions, and their resourcefulness and know-how to survive on their own in the extremes. This competence is demonstrated by spending a couple of nights in a self-constructed snow cave, downhill and cross-country skiing proficiency, ice-climbing expertise, avalanche awareness, first responder skills and mastery of orienteering.

She is competent at what is called self-arrest—the positive use of an ice ax when hurtling uncontrollably down a pitch of ice. The rescuer turns even as she falls so her head is upward with her face toward the slope. As she twirls, she drives the pick of the ice ax into the frozen surface deeply enough to stop, or arrest, her downward motion.

The winter rescuer working as a ski patroller practices ski lift rescue involving climbing and lowering passengers from stranded chairs. She is familiar with all of the lands encompassing the ski area so that she is prepared when a skier strays off the trails. This ski patroller has national certification from one of the country's ski patrol organizations, which require medical knowledge as well as skiing and wilderness expertise.

Winter survival classes are offered by groups like the Quest Survival School, 17815 Saddlewood Road, Monument, CO 80132. (719) 481-2331.

Qualifications

When at play, the extreme rescuer flies up rock cracks and hoots a lot. When at work on a rescue, as she traverses a summit, descends, then rafts in a floe-filled river to get on-scene, this child-at-heart is subdued. But she is in her world with the element of danger or death looming over her. She has learned all she knows the hard way. The excitement and enthusiasm for the job overrides the price paid in terms of pain and injuries for learning what she knows.

She is able and willing to climb for periods as long as twenty-four hours, doing so without rest as she races with the effects that winter temperatures have on the person in distress and on herself. Your rescuer will get fatigued, but recoups rapidly, ready to go for another twelve hours or twenty-five miles. She knows how to care for and feed her body, satisfing its energy demands even when she is working at far beyond her normal pace.

The Eskimo have dozens of words for snow. As rescuer extrodinaire Tim Setnika writes in the bible of winter rescue, *Wilderness Search and Rescue*, snow and ice change their consistency minute by minute, day by day and season by season. The winter rescuer must be a good observer, a historian who remembers what she has experienced in the past as the best indicator for what might happen next.

Avalanche Articles

The American Association of Avalanche Professionals produces a newsletter, *The Avalanche Review*, providing avalanche news and reports. The association can be contacted at P.O. Box 34004, Truckee, California 96160. (916) 587-6104.

Job Description

Winter rescuers working on state or federal lands or for ski areas might deal with avalanche prevention. They dig pits in the snow to analyze conditions, snowpack, and the layering to ascertain slab-stability. They use explosives to loosen potential problems before they move on.

The ski patroller who performs winter rescue in her area is expected to communicate by radio and carry it in a chest harness or in a special radio pocket of her parka. She is an advanced downhill skier who, when snowplowing down a double black diamond trail that usually she shusses—crouches over her skis, her poles tucked in her armpits—at lightening speed, can control a sled loaded with gear and a patient trailing behind her. Depending upon the difficulty of the trail, there might be a second rescuer behind serving as a brake; rescuers must be able to perform this essential skill.

Backcountry guides and rangers in winter rescue have their winter gear packed, ready to be called out. They know what they might need in any situation, and do not forget crucial equipment. This takes a serious amount of organization.

Days are shorter in the winter and, at the same time, it takes longer to get to the victim when slogging through a winter wonderland. So more than ever, rescuers need to respond without delay. Other jobs and other lives must be able to be placed on hold when there is a call out.

Equipment

The winter rescuer's regalia might include such survival toys, tools and togs as:

- rampons, which are beartrap-looking ice cleats that strap over hiking boots

This ski patrol team uses a basket stretcher to bring a victim to safety. The extended towing handles help in guiding the stretcher down the slope without harming the victim. The rear rescuer uses a foot-end tow line to assist in guiding the stretcher. (Photo used by permission of Ferno-Washington.)

- basketlike snowshoes
- downhill skis, boots and telescoping ski poles for double duty as avalanche probes and walking staffs
- cross-country skis and boots
- widemouthed (if the contents are rock-hard, you can still access fluid) water bottles stowed close to the body to prevent freezing
- high-tech materials like Gore-Tex, Tekware and Polarguard for multilayered clothing systems
- exploring and trekking shirts
- balaclava
- ear bands
- folding shovel
- performance pile jackets
- ice picks
- toilet paper
- personal first aid kit
- goggles and glare-protective glasses

This ski patrol team tows a victim to safety by attaching a trail sled basket stretcher to a snowmobile. Metal runners on the underside of the stretcher aid movement over ice. (Photo used by permission of Ferno-Washington.)

- stockings and sock liners
- day pack
- backpack
- hip belts
- sleeping bag rated to subzero temperatures with Insolite foam pad and a bivouac (nicknamed bivi) sack to slip over the sleeping bag for wind, cold and moisture protection when a tent is not available
- shoulder strap camera
- instant and freeze-dried food packets
- wax-coated matches
- ministove with high-volume fuel for melting snow

- interchangeable shells
- midlayers
- down gloves
- mittens
- finger mitts
- complete expedition layered glove systems
- thermal underwear
- windproof jackets

The Stokes litter is used often by winter rescuers. This one is shown with an impact-resistant Lexan shield to keep debris from the victim's face. The vertical-evacuation stretcher harness is attached to the litter when a victim must be hoisted to safety. (Photo © CMC Rescue, Inc., used by permission.)

- zip T-necks
- fleecewear
- mountain light overpants and jackets
- altitude jackets and bibs
- tents
- radio chest-harness to carry a two-way communication device (some jackets have such a radio pocket built-in)
- self-arresting ice ax
- helmet
- rope rescue gear

The rescuer has access to snow cats and snowmobiles, and knowledge about their capabilities and operation. Sometimes a Sked, a plastic stretcher that rolls lengthways for easy transport and cocoons the patient within it, is pulled behind. Or a Stokes litter, the rigid

---

The Well-Dressed Rescuer

D ressing for winter survival is an overriding principal. The winter mountaineer who responds to rescue operations is into layering; the trapped air between clothing-thicknesses insulates along with each clothing layer. Lightweight down (weight being an important consideration when you're carrying all of your needs on your back) loses its insulating properties when wet and is slow to dry. While wool is the warmest wet fabric, it's heavy and bulky. Certain expensive synthetics seem to offer the best compromise. They have wicking properties that keep them drier; these lighter-weight fabrics move moisture on a one-way trip away from the body. They also insulate, but not as well as wool or down.

Good winter outerwear will have zippers sewn in at the armpits, neck, waist and legs for venting water vapor away from the rescuer. These zippers keep the layers drier. Wicking and venting are important because moisture conducts heat away from the body twenty-five times faster than air.

So the choice must be made between drying ability, weight and insulation.

Note: The one thing the winter rescuer will not even consider are clothes made of cotton. This natural fabric absorbs and holds moisture, losing all insulating properties, and is slow to dry out.

Avalanche!

Avalanches are mysterious, awesome demonstrations of the powers of nature. They are winter's equivalent of a tsunami, capable of demolishing villages and anything in their path. To create an avalanche alert in your story, make sure:

- The slope is 30° to 45°.
- The slope profile is convex with a fracture line in the middle of the curve.
- There is a south-facing slope in springtime for solar gain.
- The slope is leeward so the snow will accumulate to great depths.
- The slope is smooth and open because large rocks and heavy trees can undermine your disaster by anchoring the snow.
- The snow conditions are favorable for avalanche activity. You'll want layers of different kinds of snow so that there are unstable surfaces.

If you wish to have your miscreant caught in an avalanche and survive being swept downhill and buried under tons of loose white granules, she'll have about a half hour to be found by searchers before running out of air in her tomb of snow.

orange rescue cot that is normally carried, is fastened atop a snowmobile with the patient bundled within.

Language

The names of the extensive gear list is a lexicon in itself. In addition:

CORNICE A wind-blown lip of snow easily triggered or collapsed.

CREVASSE A crack in a glacier.

DEPTH HOAR Avalanche-prone, large-grain, poorly bonded fern snow forming unstable layers.

FERN SNOW The result of degeneration of crystals into grains, which then melt together.

GRAINS Crystals of snow within a snowpack.

OLD SLIDE PATH A route that prior avalanches have followed, marked by pushed-over trees, broken limbs and a fracture line, prone to future havoc.

ROUTE SELECTION The safe choice of travel around old slide paths, on the ridge above or in the valley well below. (If your character

---

Reading Ice

Your rescuer needs to know how safe the ice is before venturing out onto it. She never assumes that, because it is frigid outside, the ice must be safe. She checks the thickness of clear, blue ice on lakes and ponds, and uses this ice strength information to understand what weight the ice can reasonably be expected to support.

Ice Thickness	Permissible Load
2"	one person on foot
3"	group, in single file
7"	passenger car
8"	light truck
10"	medium truck
12"	heavy truck

---

must go up a slide path, have him climb straight up or down; don't traverse. Unless, of course, you're looking for a disaster.)

WET GLACIER A snow-covered "river" of ice.

Dangers

The biggest peril is cold and wet, which contribute to cold challenge, stressing the body's resources. Unchecked, this medical condition advances to hypothermia.

An early sign of cold challenge working toward hypothermia is an altered mental state (written ∆MS). So your heroine-rescuer can be drawn as illogical, compounding her predicament by poor judgment. And in short order, she'll lose the wherewithal to care about herself. Hypothermic individuals typically remove their clothing, acting against their own best interests and hastening their demise.

Just as the climate stresses the people living and working in it, it also strains the natural environment. Due to alternating freezing and melting cycles, there is the danger of rock slides. Water looks safe with its hard ice coating, but it has moving water underneath. The bright, shining sun makes the air feel warm, but then the next moment there is a helacious storm. Then there are winter phenomena that don't exist in the summertime: deep snowfields, avalanches, slick icy surfaces and chunks of ice that fall from above like tombstones.

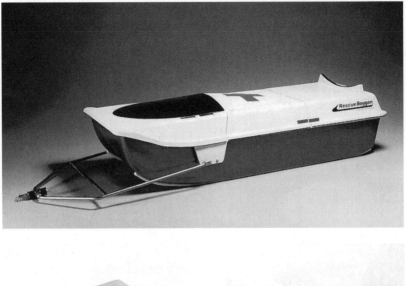

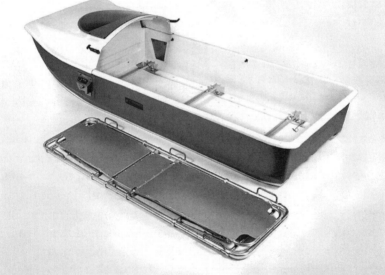

The fiberglass rescue boggan, made by Ferno, has a three-section removable canopy which completely encloses the patient, protecting the patient from harsh winter elements. (Photos used by permission of Ferno-Washington.)

CHAPTER ELEVEN

Cave Rescuer

B ecause of our animalistic survival mechanisms, we are all, to some extent, claustrophobic. So a cave rescue automatically carries with it an element of suspense with impending, unknown, scary danger. *The Handbook of Cave Rescue Operations* describes what cave rescuers, specialists who work elsewhere full time and show up when there is an emergency, encounter: "No sport has as intense an experience with an environment as does caving. On the surface, one is *on* a trail, or *on* a climb. One is very much *in* a cave with tactile stimuli . . . dampness . . . odor . . . and the vast presence of the earth pressing in as one navigates a tight crawl."

History of the Profession

Humans were dealing with the problems of caves long before buildings were collapsing and people needed vehicular extrication. No doubt cave rescuers could have been in business right back to the beginning of mankind. While caves are still used for shelter and sometimes those within them get into trouble, more often the cave rescuer is responding to a "recreational caver," no longer happy with the popular spelunker label.

Modern-times caving rescue first became a piece of popular lore when in 1925, Floyd Collins was trapped in a mine cave-in. For two weeks, the rescue party, relatives and friends were able to talk with the Kentucky miner as the work to free him continued. Press and radio coverage were intense; the incident became the sensational news story at a time when radios were in every living room. Each night, families gathered around to share with Collins his losing battle against death. Although this was a mining operation where tons of earth needed to be moved to free the victim, it nonetheless institutionalized a public perception of cave rescue.

Today's cave rescue—responding to injured or stuck recreational cavers—has become a highly technical exercise. Of all types of rescue, cave rescue is the most infrequent and the most demanding in terms of personnel. In the end, however, as with all rescue, it is one human reaching out a hand to another.

Education and Certification

The National Cave Rescue Commission (NCRC) holds an annual Cave Rescue Operations and Management Seminar attended by rescuers from all over the country. Recognizing that aspects of cave rescue overlap and relate to so many other rescue scenarios, the conference also welcomes urban search; vertical, collapse and hazmat responders; and educators and supervisors. Networking is an important aspect of the meeting.

The NCRC endorses four levels of cave rescue instruction:

1. Knots and ropes; patient packaging and maneuvering in holes and jams; systems for raising and lowering victims packaged in litters; personnel ascents and descents; communications.

2. Incident Command System (ICS); crew leadership; single rope pick offs; high-angle rescue techniques.

3. Scenarios focusing upon high- and low-angle rescue above and below grade; obstacles in water; mechanical anchoring systems; staging area set up and organization; minimum anchor equipment; mock incident.

4. Instructor course.

The National Speleological Society, over fifty years old, sponsors what they call grottos, a networking system for cavers, throughout the country. This is how cave rescuers learn their skills. They have trained through experience and by finding others to show them the ropes. Aside from technical rope work, a cave rescuer learns most of what he knows by doing.

Qualifications

Most people are claustrophobic at *some* time, whether locked in a closet or blindfolded during a game of Pin the Tail on the Donkey.

But the candidate for cave rescue can never succumb to that human frailty as he goes down into the deepest, darkest and largest caves in the United States, or crawls on his belly for hundreds of yards to locate a victim. Wherever the cave rescuer goes, he will be surrounded by absolute darkness and will constantly feel the weight of the earth pressing in on all sides.

Aside from being claustrophobic-free, he must be able to face confusion with calmness. Because the concept of being trapped alive to slowly die, reinforced by Poe and others, is not hard for any of us to imagine and dread, emotions are high when it is confirmed that a subject is snared in a cave. To conceive a plan and then follow through, the cave rescuer must rise above the tension, and be consistent and measured in his thoughts and actions.

Doing the operation right the first time, whether it is dispatching, SAR or vertical rope rescue, takes more time at the onset in order to gain minutes and sometimes hours to reach success at the end point. This is not a concept agitated individuals readily embrace. The cave rescue professional can never lose sight of it.

A cave rescuer is an amateur caver as well. This is, after all, who is knowledgeable about that environment. Who else would wish to spend time in a wild cave 1,500 feet below the earth's surface, crawling down miles-long tunnels? This brings up yet another skill: A cave rescuer is a good crawler.

Job Description

The environment the cave rescuer works within is strange, dark and dank. The unique atmosphere makes it seem as if the cave is almost breathing, with wind patterns that are relentless, intermittent, nonexistent or oscillating. Cave temperature is constant, about equal to the annual mean temperature outside the cave. There are three types of caves where the rescuer will work:

1. *Solution* Caused by water running through and dissolving carbonate rock, like limestone.

2. *Lava* Formed by molten lava and superheated gasses flowing underground, cooling and creating rooms and tunnels.

3. *Talis* Spaces and passageways within rock debris at the base of a cliff.

Lechuguilla Project

Lechuguilla Cave in New Mexico is 1,565 feet deep, the deepest in the country. It has fifty-six mapped miles, making it the third longest U.S. cave. There is an ongoing organized effort to explore, map and study the cave, which is anticipated to be more than one hundred miles long. This cave has been the site of rescues and, no doubt, will continue to be a workplace for cave rescuers.

The solution cave is the most common. It was and continues to be created by running water dissolving the rock. Inside the cave, this water will be found in conditions ranging from a slow trickle or drip to a raging underground river complete with waterfalls and deep pools.

These wet caves are carved out of softer rock, which is why the water can dissolve their floors, walls and ceilings. So the use of "aid"—the pitons, chocks, cams and webbing of rock climbing—will not hold.

The men and women who choose to rescue victims in caves are a special breed. As they noodle around exploring, they name passages, rooms and tunnels: Great White Way, Lemon Squeeze, The Rift, Corn Flakes. Below grade, they crawl, following the water, which is a cave's natural pathway construction. So the cave rescuer might have to climb up waterfalls to get where he wishes to go to stay in a carved trail.

Cave rescuers scramble frequently. This is not rock rescue, and vertical rescue is not cave rescue in reverse as one climbs down rather than up. Siphons, connections between two parts of a cave, can form a barrier and the caver will swim through these water-filled ways. All work is done in artificial light or no illumination at all, so the rescuer is not necessarily in visual communication with other crew members. And radio communication does not work well underground either. The cave rescuer is on his own.

Because caves can have miles of underground passages, the rescuer has to enjoy working with maps. Vertical drops can reach hundreds of feet, so the cave rescuer must be technical rope-rescue literate as well.

Cave rescue is an occasional event and the job description is in tandem with other rescue and emergency response responsibilities. One professional cave rescuer, a fire captain with a county fire department, has started a moonlighting business, Emergency Rescue Consultants, with another firefighter. Another professional is SCBA-certified, a regional coordinator with a SAR team and a Level IV cave rescue instructor. She serves on the board of a statewide urban SAR response team.

Equipment

The traditional spelunker hat is a helmet mounted with a brightly shining miner's lamp or a lithium, battery-driven light, which is long-lasting but heavy. For both lights, the cave rescuer carries enough illumination to shine continuously for at least twenty-four hours. A battery pack the size of a paperback book to drive the lights is fastened to the rescuer's waist, looped onto a webbing belt.

Also, butterflied over their shoulders and under their arms like a bandoleer are coils of rope. Static rope is the choice of cave rescuers as they tend to fix and leave their ropes in place, unlike high-angle rope rescuers. Accompanying that static rope are variable friction devices such as brakes and rescue-eights, which use mechanical advantage to control the weight and speed of long descents. These descenders must be sized and worked in such a way that dirt, water and grunge don't compromise their working integrity. What goes down must come up. Ascenders go along as well. They release the ascender so it does not bite the rope, then move it up the rope and tighten, pulling themselves up. Then they loosen the ascender, move it up and so on. When they do not have a load on them, ascenders slide freely. As they take the rescuer's weight, they snug up against the rope.

The rescue will be gear-intensive. But cave rescuers will not make themselves into compact efficient packhorses like rope rescuers, who have one shot to carry whatever they might need. These rescuers do a lot of handing things down and along, shuttling equipment back and forth. In tight spots, they take equipment off and push it ahead or drag it behind. Thus, cave rescue involves more support staff than rope rescue.

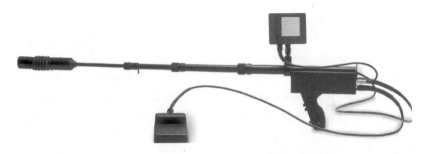

The searchcam uses a miniature, high-resolution video camera to search for victims trapped in confined spaces and collapsed structures. The telescoping probe allows visual access into difficult-to-search areas. It has been used in many high-profile emergency operations, such as the Oklahoma City bombing. It can be a valuable tool in cave rescues. (Photo © CMC Rescue, Inc., used by permission.)

An extension of rope use is a ladder, whether solid, coiled cable or rope. Ladders are an accepted part of cave rescue gear. Sometimes a ladder is quicker and more efficient than rope rigging.

Wet suits are worn for warmth in, say, a 50° solution cave with standing, running and dripping water. Unlike rope rescuers in their fashion-coordinated outfits, cave rescuers tend to be dirty and scruffy-looking. Their clothing is usually torn and takes lots of abuse.

A compass and available maps of the cave are securely placed within the rescuer's pocket.

Because a Sked litter's compactness—it can be rolled up and carried as a tube, then used to package a patient with its sides curled around the legs, arms and trunk—is coupled with a smooth exterior that allows it to slip along the ground, it is the favored litter within the small spaces of cave rescue. When in use, the bright orange, cigar-shaped cot is no bigger than the patient herself and can be raised sideways, upright or upside down.

Language

The term spelunker, or caver, is from the Latin *spelunca* or Greek *spelynx*, which means cave.

What the spelunking rescuer might encounter in the cave and have to work around are stalactites and stalagmites, carbonate icicle-shaped geologic processes. The first dangles from the cave's ceiling and forms as water drips down off the growing cone. The stalagmite is a mound built up from the ground as water drips from the ceiling. Both are formed as carbonate of lime separates out of the water solution. As the water runs off, the lime remains and forms this structure. Stalagmites and stalactites form from the same drip and eventually join together.

Dangers

A constant for cavers, and for their rescuers, is falling debris. Boulders drop and land on bodies, breaking heads and bones. Loose, rocky soil causes twisted ankles and knees. At dawn and dusk, watch out for bats!

In addition, the rescuer never forgets that the cave is a harsh environment with steep faces, confined spaces and underground rivers, all cut off from the "real" world and in total darkness to boot. This never-changing cold dungeon, with the echoing of dripping water, is unforgiving. There are no resources to draw from in this empty sphere.

Cave rescue is not one of the most dangerous rescue professions. A big storm will not come along; fire is not a threat; there are not lots of pitches to fall off of; there is time in the water, but nowhere like a dive rescuer's exposure; there are not bystanders causing difficulties; he is not on a helo about to crash. The surroundings are stable. As long as the rescuer can deal with a cave on its terms, he'll be fine.

CHAPTER TWELVE

Search-and-Rescue Team

Search as both an organized and unorganized activity has been around as long as man has looked for anything new, different or valuable. What's peculiar about our present definition is that it focuses upon a person or people as the object of the search. It is a rescue or lifesaving mission, often driven by an equal mix of altruism and adventure.

The science of search is ignored or given short shrift in movies and books. Someone is either found or not, with little information about time frames and techniques. There has been significant research effort taken to understand what works and what fails when a person is lost and it is largely unknown outside of the SAR community.

The newest aspect of SAR, urban search, is most often in connection with mass casualty incidents (MCI) such as building explosions. When a child is lost in a city, depending upon the setting, SAR teams might be mobilized. If the toddler in your story gets lost in a city park or in a neighborhood along a river, you can write in professional teams who would work in much the same way they do in a wilderness setting. When the door-to-door search is necessary, you might wish to place law enforcement at the helm; they will wish to handle this aspect within their jurisdiction to limit risk exposure.

As the public's expectations have changed, so has the SAR business. Even when volunteers do the work, there is significant cost attached to a SAR mission. At the same time, the price is going up as new technologies offer more efficient searches for more money, and as the modern-day rusticators—the weekend outdoor adventurers—expect to be rescued. This notion probably causes him to take more risks.

Charging for SAR call outs goes against most rescuers' grain. But the other side of the coin is that everyone pays when there is the need for a search. SAR teams still grapple with these issues.

History of the Profession

The exploits of some of the earliest untrained searchers are recorded in the Bible, where the SAR recruits were angels who rarely had trouble getting the lost back on track.

Although there have always been individuals or groups who would forge out in search of overdue travelers, we have to look to Europe for the first recorded corps of organized searchers. There, in the middle 900s, Bernard of Menthon dedicated his life to helping the thousands of travelers who struggled through the passes of the Swiss Alps. The career of the eventually sainted Bernard culminated in the establishment of the famed Great St. Bernard's Hospice, some 8,500 feet up in the Alps. There monks and Saint Bernard dogs rendered guidance and aid to tenth-century travelers traversing the high mountain passes. When these pilgrims went astray, missed trails, were swept down couloirs by avalanches or became famished and frozen, the searchers and their trustworthy canines located and helped them by providing food, water, warmth and shelter. From the 900s through today, the monks and dogs of the St. Bernard's Hospice remain active, and the Swiss Alps provide a playing field for constant practice.

In the 1800s, when modern alpinism emerged as a sport rather than a means of passage through mountains, the result was an increase in the numbers of lost climbers. More and more people on the continent and in the mountains of America became, in Daniel Boone's phrase, "bewildered," turned around in the wilds. They weren't necessarily lost, but they sure didn't know their way home.

In response, resident climbing guides organized their own informal SAR teams. These squads focused on the technical aspects of

Chemical lightsticks are sometimes used during nighttime search-and-rescue operations. The sparkproof sticks attach to a rescuer's buckles or zippers and burn for as long as twelve hours. (Photo © CMC Rescue, Inc., used by permission.)

mountain rescue, for example, lowering themselves down to find a climber on some distant elevated ledge. Inevitably these same groups became involved in searches because they were well equipped, physically fit to cover long distances and able to bivouac out on the trail when necessary.

In the U.S., mountain clubs, regional governments, national parks and the federal military services all began training and equipping their own SAR teams as a way of looking after their own and dealing with the increasing hordes of unprepared individuals who flocked to the woods and wildlands as a way of cleansing their souls. Angels were no longer on standby. Someone had to oversee SAR even though the physical and financial costs of search had spiraled through the 1980s and 1990s.

What has evolved is a two-tiered system of search. At the bottom is a vast network of rescue professionals not trained in search who, nonetheless, find themselves in charge of local, short-term searches. Loosely under the command of these leaders is a motley crew of firefighters, Boy and Girl Scouts, civilian volunteers recruited from surrounding neighborhoods and, occasionally, National Guard recruits. All of these enthusiastic helpers should be written in as inexperienced. The best that you can suggest they can do is to stay in a rough line in sight of one another as they sweep through a section of woods or field. At worst, because of their lack of training, you can feel confident that you're being accurate if you have them obliterating clues, masking or destroying scent trails and draining valuable resources.

At the top of the search system there is a small cadre of professional searchers. Many have their own particular expertise such as dog handling or technical climbing. They are organized into teams, some volunteer and some paid, and connected by a loose network of telephones, radios and pagers. The one characteristic that connects these teams is a delight in the adventure, a willingness to sacrifice large chunks of time in often fruitless searches.

Education and Certification

Nationally recognized SAR certification is offered by NASAR through their "Fundamentals of Search and Rescue" (FUNSAR) course. Content material that is covered includes terrain evaluation, behavioral profiling, math for searches, probability density and search planning. Other NASAR courses lead to certification as an SAR Tech I, II and III, and SAR Tech Evaluator.

Line searching, Northumberland Rain Dance search technique and grid searching will be taught (see "Job Description" section for descriptions), along with its five subsets: sound sweep, standard sweep, high-visibility sweep, low-visibility sweep and body sweep. Orienteering must be mastered. SAR team members will be trained in helicopter rescue techniques. In addition to hands-on training, the didactic portion of the course will give insight into

> ### State of the Art
> Rural states and those with significant open land might offer state-wide SAR certification. Maine Search and Rescue (MESAR) offers a course along the lines of the NASAR training. Oregon's certification program includes education in winter survival, equipment operations, public education, survival techniques, map and compass use, and outdoor and water safety.

the psychology of the lost individual and statistical probabilities.

Depending upon the team's location—near woodlands, inland waters or an ocean—classes in winter trekking, desert survival or mountain climbing might be completed. Appropriate clothing and gear will be discussed and understood. In areas with specific types of disasters such as earthquakes, tsunamis and flooding, courses and training will be conducted on SAR techniques for those specific disasters.

NASAR has an annual seminar, "Response," offering guidance and skills training in the form of workshops, panel discussions and demonstrations. This meeting brings together the movers and shakers from the SAR community as well as rescue professionals in related fields.

Qualifications
Familiarity with the local terrain and personal survival is essential or the rescuer becomes another subject. Knowledge of local weather patterns and conditions, and how to work within them is expected.

In addition to a knowledge of the environment, the successful SAR rescuer:
- Is able to navigate
- Knows an array of specialized search techniques and is able to teach them to volunteers
- Has the ability to manage the injured or distressed subject distant from normal care resources
- Has the endurance to successfully move persons through hostile environments

---

Overdue Person!

Maine's Wilderness Rescue Team's call-out system is typical of those used for the numeric pagers team members might carry. In this case, 43 through 47 are geographic divisions of the state:

Urgency	Type	Location
01-urgent	11-technical rescue	41-Baxter Park
02-when available	12-search	42-Acadia Park
03-standby/no	13-dog teams	43-Gray
callback	14-plane crash	44-Sydney
000000-test	15-major disaster	45-Greenville
888888-mission	16-backup needed	46-Bangor
ended	17-water rescue	47-Ashland
999999-canceled	18-medical	

The SAR community salutes itself through several annual awards to qualified rescuers. The Hal Foss Award is for significant contribution to SAR, as are the Valor Award, the NASAR Service Award, the State/Province SAR Awards and the NASAR Instructor Award.

Job Description

In some senses, the trained professional searcher, a member of a SAR team, is always at work no matter what she does in the real world. Whether an accountant, an architect or a plumber, she always has at hand a pack filled with gear, including food to get her through forty-eight hours alone in the wilderness. Depending upon the activity level of her search team, this pack may live in a closet at home or stuffed into the trunk of an auto.

This searcher wears a beeper or pager. Any time, day or night, the tone is liable to go off with numbers flashing across the little screen. Sometimes the call out will be a phone number; other times the message will be encoded to convey the type of search, urgency and approximate location. This original message and subsequent brief phone call to the team leader will provide information necessary for the searcher to put her life on hold for a day or two and then head for the rendezvous spot.

The searcher is on duty when she attends regular monthly meetings of her team. Sometimes the team will deal with administrative details of team operations. Other times the team might take a whole day and stage a mock search, complete with victim and clues, to practice skills and coordination. Such practice drills give team members familiarity with the surrounding wildlands where real searches are most liable to be conducted.

When the call comes out, the searcher will drive to the assigned search headquarters. This may be a local high school, a park headquarters or even two coordinates on a map. It depends upon the point last seen (PLS) of the victim and the availability of resources. Generally, however, by the time a professional searcher has been called, the search is the real thing and enough time has passed that the search team can count on a significant investment of time.

Search headquarters will be much like a military camp. For a full-blown search, depending upon the site, rooms or tents will have been assigned for feeding and sleeping, planning and public relations, and mapping and logistics. An individual search team will usually be joined by several other teams, each with specific assignments. All of these spaces and teams will ideally be run with military precision by the search manager or, when under the ICS, by the incident commander (IC) and the various components of ICS.

The searcher's first on-scene activity will be a briefing session run by the IC. Here, teams will learn the latest information on the progress of the search:

- Who is the victim? What was he last wearing? PLS? Special physical or mental problems?
- What areas and sectors have already been searched? With what success?
- Are there any new clues?
- What's the weather forecast for the next twenty-four to forty-eight hours? Any especially dangerous conditions? Are there other environmental dangers or topographic conditions to be aware of?
- Communications formats and schedules.
- Assignments for each team.

A trained searcher and her team might be assigned to conduct any one of three distinct kinds of searches. The specific assignment is dependent upon the duration of the search, the location and meaning of clues recently found, and the estimated present-time condition of the victim.

Class I Search

If the team is assigned a Class I Search, it is expected to rapidly search specific areas where there is a high probability of finding clues about the subject. The team might be asked to fan out and follow a known or suspected trail the subject was on. They might be asked to follow likely routes such as drainages, old logging roads, ridge lines and the likes that the subject might come across and decide to follow.

In all of these efforts, the team will be highly clue-conscious. The operating assumption is that the subject is still conscious and will respond to the noise and sight of searchers. The team is spread out, looking for clues; if the subject finds them, then so much the better. The team is also working hard to finish each segment of a Class I search quickly and efficiently. If following a trail, it will send runners ahead, leapfrogging the team's position and looking for fresh signs. If they find a clue, then the team will move up quickly, often skipping great distances of tedious clue searching.

At the end of a Class I search, the team reports what they found—a scarf, a cold campfire, a Hershey bar wrapper—and, equally important, where they found it. This information is transferred to the ICS overhead map and is used to further narrow subsequent search operations. If the team found no clues or sign of the subject, their efforts were not wasted. On the contrary, this tells the overhead team that there is a high likelihood that the subject was never in the areas searched. Knowing where somebody is not is important. A sector can then be ignored, and areas beyond it as well. The field has been narrowed and person power can be utilized in sectors that continue to be active.

Class II Search

A Class II search substitutes efficiency for speed. The subject is still assumed to be responsive but by this point, the search is narrowing. The presence of earlier-found clues has pointed in the direction of particular sectors for a more thorough search. Occasionally the terrain is so densely vegetated that a Class I search would not have penetrated it, but the area is still a likely place for the victim to be.

For this search pattern, the team does a grid search. They are assigned a specific area and conduct their search in a line, starting from one known point and ending at a second. The spacing of their line will be dependent upon the IC's evaluation of search progress and conditions, and the desired probability of detection (POD) of the particular search segment. The closer together the searchers are spaced and the more time they spend searching a specific area, the higher the POD.

According to NASAR calculations, it takes a trained grid-searching team 3½ hours to advance one mile. If searchers are spaced 180 feet apart, then about thirty searchers can cover a square mile in 3½ hours. They will have a 10 percent chance of finding the subject. If, however, the searchers are stationed only twenty feet apart, they will have a 90 percent chance of finding the subject. However, the team would need 264 members to cover the same square mile in 3½ hours.

Once their spacing is established, the team lines up along a known feature like a flag line or road. On command, the line advances into the search sector. Searchers at each end of the line mark with fluorescent flagging tape the edges of their search area. It is critical that the searchers be able to tell the overhead team exactly what they searched and where this area is on the overhead map. If it cannot be identified, the SAR team's efforts were useless. If they found clues but do not know where they were, their efforts were worse than useless. In large searches involving volunteers and pros, this is a constant problem. It creates chaos, the arch enemy of an organized search.

Interior members of the line have two responsibilities. They must maintain the assigned distance from their partners on either side, and must not overlook clues as they move forward. Some teams hold rigidly to their spacing, while heads and eyes flick back and forth looking for clues. Other teams have adopted a technique called "purposeful wandering," which encourages line searchers to explore the nooks and crannies within their corridor.

Team leaders will follow behind the line. Their job is to evaluate clues; locate on a map where they were found and note the time when they were spotted; and stay in radio contact with search management. They use their eyes, compass and map to ensure the entire line stays on course and searches the assigned area. As the line progresses, if one of the searchers kneels to examine a broken limb or simply to tie a shoe, the whole line is stopped by the team leader's whistle or with a "Halt!" Movement will not be renewed until everyone is ready and the spacing has been restored.

Class III Search

If the IC believes the lost person is no longer responsive or, because of clues found, the subject is in a particular area, a Class III search will be ordered. Class III is a Class II with tighter line spacing. If earlier searches employed first speed and then efficiency, a Class III search aims for thoroughness.

It is slow and systematic. Depending upon the ruggedness of the land and vegetative cover, line spacing might be as little as ten feet, which means that each searcher is responsible for just five and a half feet of terrain on each side of her.

When a Class III search's segment is completed, the overhead team can be reasonably certain the LP is not in that area and any clues will have been found. This is a thorough search technique.

One interesting way to describe your SAR team's designation of spacing is to depict them joining in on the Northumberland Rain Dance. A mock clue is dropped on the ground, something that approximates what the SAR team is searching for. It might be as large and obvious as a body wearing a red parka or as small as a Dentyne gum wrapper dropped by a known-to-be-chewing LP.

The team then forms a tight circle around the stand-in for the missing object/person and begins to circle it, conducting the Northumberland Rain Dance. Individuals move in and out, nearer and farther away from the object, but always keeping it just in sight as they circle around it. Once a distance is determined where everyone can see the object, the spacing for the search has been decided. The Northumberland Rain Dance is precise enough that

> ### *Searcher Spacing*
>
> Terrain and ground cover dictate the size of search segments and searcher spacing.
>
> - A standard segment size for a half-day search is 100 to 250 acres.
> - It will take ten to twelve searchers at a nonthorough spacing (100 feet) to search 160 acres in about four hours. In comparison, a dog team will take two to six hours to search 160 acres.
> - Trained grid searchers spaced 100 feet apart in moderately dense underbrush will find five out of ten objects; POD = 50 percent.
> - Spaced 60 feet apart, they will find seven out of ten objects; POD = 70 percent.
> - Spaced 20 feet apart, they will find nine out of ten objects; POD = 90 percent.
> - Suspect any team that completes their assigned search in half the time.

the team leader and the IC can be certain that even the smallest clues will be spotted.

Sometimes search management will have a team search an area more than once. Often it is expedient to do two Class II searches at right angles with wide line spacing rather than a single Class III search. The probabilities of detection are comparable.

Most searches are on foot, but both mounted SAR personnel and mountain bike teams have been used in searches compatible with these modes of transportation. Three-person mountain bike teams should be depicted working with the efficiency and speed of a wide-tired, four-wheel-drive, all-terrain vehicle (ATV), but with greater maneuverability and without damage to the environment.

Whether on foot, using ATVs or mountain bikes or on horseback, at the conclusion of each sector of an efficient, well-run search, the search professional and her team will return to search headquarters for debriefing. The IC/search manager will want to know all of the details: what was found or not located; the nature of the terrain searched; how the searchers feel about the POD in that area. This information defines decisions for the activities of the next shift.

The following pages show an EMS cross-trained team of firefighters using a two-piece basket stretcher to rescue an injured victim. The basket is easy to store, carry and assemble. See illustrations on pages 174, 175 and 176. (Photo used by permission of Ferno-Washington.)

Equipment

Rangers, sheriffs and state police receive calls from turned-around hikers who don't know where they are or where they have been. Hopefully, after the lost individual describes his surroundings, he can be given instructions to lead him to a road or other landmark toward civilization. As the technology continues to advance, this high-tech form of SAR where the searcher and subject never see one another will become commonplace. Accordingly, cell phones have become standard issue for SAR professionals.

(Photo used by permission of Ferno-Washington.)

These kinds of telecommunication in SAR join with global positioning systems (GPS) to change the face of SAR. The handy GPS devices now allow the lost person with a cell phone to give his coordinates! GPS helps the SAR team in the field as well. Each member's exact position is monitored through GPS and automatic packet reporting systems (APRS).

But compared to some other rescue professions, SAR teamwork is not equipment-intensive. A backpack, hiking clothes and gear, a good pair of boots and appropriately layered clothing against changes in weather are what is necessary. SAR team members carry a compass, map, emergency kit in the event that they themselves get lost, and enough food, water and weather protection to get them

(Photo used by permission of Ferno-Washington.)

through twenty-four hours exposed to the elements. The emergency kit includes waxed matches, signaling devices including a whistle and mirror, six feet of parachute cord and personal necessities such as extra contact lenses or medications.

The International Search and Rescue Trade Association's (INSARTA) newsletter is a source of product and equipment information. This publication also gives a sense of the fieldwork of SAR, including training schedules, description of recent searches and their outcomes, and cutting-edge technology. INSARTA can be contacted at 4537 Foxhall Drive NE, Olympia, Washington 98516; (206) 624-1585.

(Photo used by permission of Ferno-Washington.)

Dangers

There are the obvious environmental hazards associated with SAR. After all, professional searchers are in the field because someone else has already managed to get himself into trouble in the same area. But most search is done in close proximity to other team members, and everyone is looking out for each other. As a result, search can be long and tedious, but is rarely dangerous to the searcher.

If the teams are not professional SAR teams, the most common problem is getting turned around. Untrained volunteers constantly get lost, adding to the number of LP and to the general confusion.

Those Who Stabilize

CHAPTER THIRTEEN

First Responder

A rmed with the least amount of training and equipped with the tools to do the most amount of good, first responders are the foot soldiers of field medicine. They exist because there is a striking correlation between the start of medical help and patient outcome. The sooner a patient gets help, especially when his injuries or illness are life-threatening, the greater his likelihood of survival.

In the field, the first responder has but two jobs: to get on-scene quickly because he lives or works nearby; and to begin the treatment process by stabilizing the patient, the first goal in the emergency department as well. Providing this immediate care is the role of the first responder.

The war against accidental death and disability is won when there are first responders scattered throughout the community, holding the fort until the heavy artillery, in the form of EMTs, paramedics and the ambulance, arrives. First responders are a piece of the emergency package in the thick of the action, whether the setting is rural, urban or the wilderness.

History of the Profession

In 1797, Napoleon implemented a program designed to triage or evaluate wounded on the battlefield and then transport them to medical aid stations behind the lines. Choices were made about soldiers deemed saveable and those who were not; who was deserving of prompt care and who could wait. Patients were transported in wooden carts, some horsedrawn and some pulled by hand. This prehospital system, as crude as it was, today is acknowledged as the first example of an emergency medical system. The soldiers who

> ## Early Ambulance Responses
>
> In 1865, Commercial Hospital (now University Hospital in Cincinnati) put an ambulance into service. Its driver was paid $360 per year. Bellevue Hospital in Manhattan fielded an ambulance in 1869. By 1891, Bellevue was responding to 4,392 calls a year and carried the following equipment: one quart of brandy, two tourniquets, six bandages, six sponges, splint materials, blankets, a two-ounce bottle of persulphate of iron, handcuffs and a straightjacket.

risked life and limb to rescue the wounded from battlefields are properly considered to be the *first* responders.

For the next one hundred and twenty years, there were few improvements in the triage and transport system that Napoleon devised. Civilian ambulance services had been started in Cincinnati and New York City in the 1860s and there were transport systems developed to deal with some of the carnage on Civil War battlefields, but these ventures remained small. Their focus continued to be upon transport to what is called definitive care which, at that time, was the hospital.

In the 1920s, several volunteer rescue squads formed. A number were along the New Jersey seacoast. These lifesaving stations were dedicated to saving victims of swimming accidents and shipwrecks. In Roanoke, Virginia, a different kind of rescue service was organized. This squad generally is credited with being the first EMS unit in the country. Today there is a national EMS repository, the To the Rescue Museum in Virginia, which honors the pioneering work of Julian Stanley Wise and his rescue squad.

The story goes that, as a young child, Wise helplessly stood by as two men drowned in a river accident in Roanoke. Haunted by this memory, he organized a rescue team to respond to river accidents. His team members were equipped with matching swimsuit uniforms and whatever gear they could buy, borrow or make. They were volunteers and, when called, would run from home or work to the rescue scene.

Wise had a canny sense for organization and publicity. He raised funds from the city and used local newspapers to build recognition and support. Over the years, his rescue stations grew in size and number. They also began to expand in scope of practice. Automobile accidents and attendant trauma gave Wise and his cohorts plenty to deal with through the 1930s and 1940s. What remained special about Wise and the Roanoke crews was that they always recognized the need to treat on-scene, to stabilize their patients before transporting them to the local hospitals. Wise's work and ideas were picked up by other communities and individuals (it does not diminish Wise to acknowledge that he also was good at self-promotion) and rescue squads sprang up throughout Virginia. To this day in Virginia and surrounding areas, the tradition is to call ambulance services rescue squads.

In the rest of the country, care of the sick and the injured had taken a different direction. Enterprising funeral directors, who had the vehicles with long enough beds to carry people on stretchers, began to transport the still-living to a hospital for additional care. Funeral directors responded to the scene of a car accident and, depending upon what they found, turned their sign around, changing the hearse to an ambulance or vice versa.

The mortuaries' hold on the business loosened with the 1966 National Research Council of the National Academy of Sciences' White Paper, "Accidental Death and Disability: The Neglected Disease of Modern Society." Federal legislation in the form of the Highway Safety Act of 1966 was not far behind. The EMS system was born within the Department of Transportation.

Spurred by seed money from the feds and private grants, local EMS systems grew in stature and importance. In Pittsburgh, the local black community, tired of inadequate care from existing services and funeral directors, organized their own EMS system. This Freedom House program evolved into Pittsburgh EMS, a system that still leads the nation in response and innovation.

In the first national rush to establish EMS, first responders like the Virginia rescue programs were going to be left in the lurch unless they began to train their providers as EMS responders. Ambulances were purchased. Necessary radio communications gear was bought.

Like Wise's rescue squads, first responders located throughout the community offered EMS programs the ability to get help on-scene quickly to triage and stabilize the patient while more advanced EMS units were on the way. In short, FRs took giant strides toward reducing deaths and disabilities.

Today these different levels of EMS response arriving on-scene at different times and with skills and equipment is called *tiered response*. It is the norm in the majority of EMS systems.

First responders have evolved into three distinct branches of stabilizing medical response:

1. ***Wilderness*** These first responders, nicknamed wofers for WFR, tend to be guides, group leaders and outdoor counselor-types. Their work leaves them likely to come upon remote medical emergencies where they will spend long periods of time with their patients either awaiting the arrival of higher-licensed care and transportation, or performing arduous and lengthy patient transports to get to definitive care. Their EMS training is one piece of their overall job responsibilities. They are also skilled outdoors leaders and have as part of their wofer course at least rudimentary training in several technical, accessing rescue skills.

2. ***Suburban and rural*** This first responder is a local shopkeeper, artist, retired pharmacist, secretary with a community-minded boss or college student, all citizens with control over their work, family or school schedules. With jump kits in the backs of their vehicles and radios or beepers on their hips, they are able to drop what they are doing at a moment's notice. During suburban and rural emergencies, where distances are great and ambulance response times slow, first responders are a neighborhood or small town extension of the regional EMS service. They are the direct, in-line descendants of Julian Stanley Wise and his Roanoke Rescue Squad. Frequently volunteers, FRs are a valuable asset to the smaller communities they serve as a breeding ground for EMTs, paramedics, nurses and doctors. They make interesting potential characters who, once exposed to the heady activities of the professional medical provider, might find the course of their lives changed by this experience.

3. **Urban**   EMS systems in urban areas first began utilizing first responders in the late 1980s. The idea was to cross-train firefighters in an effort to obtain faster EMS response times and, not coincidentally, to get more bang for the buck of municipal payrolls. When this tiered-response system was demonstrated to save lives, some cities also trained police as first responders. By the mid-nineties, 32 percent of the nation's largest municipalities used first-responder firefighters and police based in neighborhood stations to supplement their EMS programs.

Some cities also tried upgrading care and saving money within their quick response models. They began dispatching a medic in a specially equipped Jeeplike vehicle. This urban first responding medic would size up the scene, diagnose the problem, call for other advanced life support (ALS) providers, or decide less expensive basic life support (BLS) care would be sufficient and appropriate. These medical professionals, confusingly referred to as first responders, are paramedics. Unlike the first responder, these ALS providers are the top of the medical rescue tree in terms of education, responsibility and licensure. The BLS first responder is at the entry level.

Education and Certification

Usually first responders are certified (which has to do with successful completion of training) and licensed (permission to practice pre-hospital medicine) by state EMS boards, although some areas handle this process on a county, city or hospital district level. Information on licensing procedures in a particular area can be obtained by contacting the state EMS office.

Training consists of a course usually offered during evenings and on Saturdays over a couple of months. The forty-hour program covers the objectives of the U.S. Department of Transportation's First Responder Curriculum and includes didactic and practical hands-on instruction, examinations and in-hospital internship opportunities. Either as part of their EMS training or as a prerequisite for entrance into the FR training, all FRs must be licensed in CPR by the Red Cross, the American Heart Association or their equivalent.

As an FR, your character will have BLS skills to deal with the ABCs of medicine: A—maintaining the patient's airway so oxygen flows in and out of the lungs; B—assist breathing when the patient cannot maintain sufficient respirations; and C—ensure blood circulation to vital organs. Your hero will work in the field responding to farm, environmental and industrial accidents; delivering babies; bandaging and splinting; assessing diabetic and cardiac emergencies; and operating the ambulance and their radios.

In less populated areas, first responders might go on a call, care for the patient at the side of the EMTs and medics and drive the ambulance. The Department of Transportation's Emergency Vehicle Operator Course (EVOC) and Ambulance training, a sixteen-hour course, includes the basic aspects of communications, ambulance types and normal operations. Actual practice driving time is included.

EMTs above the first-responder level supervise the patient packing, loading and care upon transport.

First responders know how to use an automatic external defibrillator (AED). This is a device that, when someone dies, shocks the heart to stop its useless fluttering. Once stilled, it is hoped the heart muscle will reorganize, then start in a more normal rhythm that will at least pump some oxygen-containing blood around the body.

Qualifications

The first responder's training emphasizes improvisational skills and calmness in crisis situations. Unlike the fully equipped, sterile emergency department with helpers at one's elbow, the world of the field responder is full of risk, challenge, excitement and reward.

The first responding licensure is entry level. A good citizen-character would get involved in EMS, find the work fascinating and go on to license up to EMT or even paramedic.

Job Description

First responders, whether in the woods, on the water or in a warehouse, must react calmly, quickly and safely to an emergency. EMS systems have different methods of scheduling to guarantee this response.

Shock, Shock, Shock!

To defibrillate, two paddles (or sticky electro-pads with some models) are held against the chest. One is below the middle of the right collarbone; the other is on the ribs well beneath the left armpit. These paddles "read" the heart's rhythm and see if it is one of the two rhythms that can be shocked back to a normal, lub-dubbing beat. A heart is *de*fibrillated because it is fibrillating—wiggling and squirming chaotically and unproductively like a bucket of worms—and the muscle mass needs to be reorganized because the wiggly, Jell-O-like heart is not pumping blood and needed oxygen throughout the body. When a patient is in need of defibbing, he is dead. Once it is determined that the heart is fibrillating, the defib builds up a charge and, upon command (either automatically by the defibrillator or when the medical provider depresses a button), the defibrillator discharges a surge of electricity (200 to 360 joules) from paddle to paddle and through the heart.

For the heart, this shock is akin to throwing a bucket of water at a hysterical person. It stops all activity and provides an opportunity to reorganize calmly and efficiently. The hope is that the heart's electrical controls will reorganize themselves and establish a rhythm compatible with life. If the first defibrillation is unsuccessful, a second and third shock will be administered. This sequence of three shocks may be repeated several times until success or until it is determined that the victim is beyond electrical resuscitation.

Before each defibrillation, the medical provider calls out, "Clear, clear, everybody clear." Anybody touching the patient is at risk of also getting defibrillated. In the world of EMS, stories are legion about providers who were accidentally shocked and seriously injured or killed by a stray current. Once, at a baseball game, when responders defibrillated a patient in the bleachers, they accidentally shocked a number of fans sitting on the same metal bleachers as the patient.

Suburban and rural services might radio an alerting sound, called a tone, followed by the patient's sex, age, chief complaint and location. The closest FR who can respond notifies dispatch. Or the FR may be scheduled to cover specific areas during particular time frames. One FR might respond from his home after work; another may choose to be available forty-eight hours over the weekend; a third may be on duty from the office during working hours. In all

---

Size Up

A first responder, after checking the scene for safety, understands whether he has a trauma case or a medical problem. Trauma is something that impacts the body from an outside source. Medical ills are in response to happenings within the body. The first responder must decide what resources need to be called in.

Next, the FR performs an initial assessment. He wants to know the patient's level of consciousness (LOC), and checks the airway, breathing and circulation or heartbeat. This is done by taking the patient's pulse.

He then performs a physical exam (PE). He will look for DOTS: *Deformities* such as angulated bones. Are there any *Open* injuries? What about *Tenderness*? Or *Swelling*?

Once he has an idea of the patient's condition, he will continue to assess and reassess for changes. This is called the ongoing assessment.

---

cases, the FR must carry a beeper or radio and, depending upon the service's protocols, be available.

While urban FRs are dispatched as a part of their normal duty and have short runs, wofers are ready to hike a few hundred yards or even twenty miles to get to the scene. The time commitment for a wilderness response ranges from two hours to several days. With their always stowed-and-ready medical backpack, wofers must keep survival gear including food and water sufficient for forty-eight hours (see the "Equipment" section).

Once on scene, the immediate duty of all first responders is to stabilize—to make sure that things don't go downhill. First they assess or figure out what is going on and why, and determine: Is the scene safe? FRs must understand that a hurt rescuer becomes a drain on already-limited medical resources. Responders who rush to save someone while endangering themselves and others are considered heros only by the media.

Crowd control, weapons and domestic violence are a few of the scene safety issues FRs confront. They must be ready to don personal protection gear (PPG) whenever there is the risk of contamination from hepatitis, tuberculosis or AIDS. No matter what the danger, the FR is charged with making the scene safe, which might

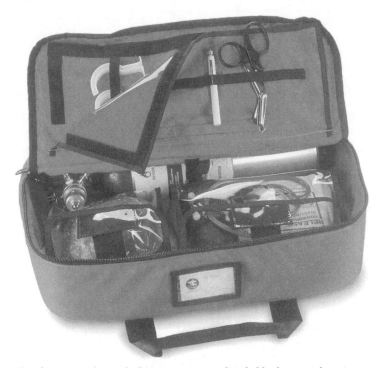

This first responder pack, known as a jump kit, holds the crucial equipment needed for emergency response. Notice the various divided areas, which help the responder stay organized during an emergency. (Photo © CMC Rescue, Inc., used by permission.)

include standing back and waiting for a police response.

Once assured of scene safety, first responders assess the victim, fixing whatever they can fix. They collect a patient history and convey relevant information to en route EMTs and medics. The first responder must be comfortable operating and communicating over a hand-held portable radio, and must have medical knowledge and language to describe the patient's chief complaint, signs and symptoms, condition and vital signs.

As EMTs and medics arrive, the FR's role changes from leader to gofer. The FR assists in treatment and helps package the patient for transport. Once the patient is in transit, the FR cleans the scene, ties up loose ends and goes back to an interrupted life. The municipal FR heads back to the station.

FRs keep current with innovations in the field of emergency medicine and maintain their licensure through continuing medical education (CME), workshops and retesting. A typical amount of continuous medical training might include in a year's time six hours of basic medical courses, six hours of basic trauma instruction and an additional ten hours in accepted medical education.

Equipment

FRs must always carry either a beeper or a radio. They can never be more than a few feet away from the tone and voice of dispatch. They have to know where to go and what to expect when they get there. Well-equipped FRs carry a radio to communicate with dispatch and to advise the responding ambulance with EMTs what to expect and what additional equipment or other rescue personnel is needed.

The second piece of essential FR gear is his jump kit: the bag where he stores all of his trusted medical tools and equipment. Jump kits are hard, plastic boxes, often adapted from fishing tackle boxes. Or they are canvas or nylon bags with lots of clips, pockets and fabric divisions within. On the outside of either case or kit is at least an EMS star of life and a squad emblem. The jump kit will be bursting with:

- activated charcoal
- bag valve mask—infant/ped
- binoculars
- BP cuff/stethoscope
- BSI hand wipes
- BSI isolation kit, mask and suit
- burn kit
- Chux pad
- elastic bandages
- EMT scissors
- flashlight
- foil blanket
- gauze pads/4×4; 3×3; 2×2
- glucose tube
- glycerine swabs
- hazmat guide

- Kling
- latex gloves
- locator book
- nasal cannula
- notepad
- OB kit
- oral A/W kit
- oral thermometer
- O_2 cylinder and tubing
- pen/pencil
- pocket mask
- portable suction
- run sheet
- SAM splint
- sterile water/irrigating
- suction catheter
- tape
- tissues
- trauma pad
- triangular bandages

In urban systems, which often can afford better and more expensive equipment, FRs might also carry the AED for use within four to six minutes of the heart stopping. FRs shock chaotic hearts so they'll straighten up, restoring life-giving circulation to the victim of a heart attack.

Language

It is not just the FR who checks the ABCs of medicine. So does the surgeon, the paramedic in the field, the emergency room nurse, the pediatrician. It is a basic medical protocol or standard order of conducting a medical assessment. The A stands for airway. Here are the buzzwords that tie in:

AIRWAY The windpipe, or trachea, which is the route oxygen takes from the nose and mouth into the lungs.

AIRWAY OBSTRUCTION Blockage in the windpipe, which is the route oxygen needs to take for the patient to stay alive.

CYANOSIS When oxygen does not reach the lungs, thereby not reaching the heart and bloodstream, the body turns blue. This can first be apparent in the nail beds.

HEAD TILT/CHIN LIFT Positioning the head so that rescue breathing's oxygen will shoot straight down the trachea or windpipe.

RESCUE BREATHING Gently blowing the rescuer's unused expelled oxygen into the patient's mouth by using a pocket mask, which presses over the victim's mouth like a toilet plunger. The rescuer breathes into a one-way valved mouthpiece.

RESPIRATORY ARREST Breathing has stopped. Cardiac arrest will occur in seconds unless rescue breathing begins.

RESPIRATORY DISTRESS Difficulty breathing.

Dangers

First responding to unstable scenes can be unsafe. It is the FR's responsibility to size up the scene and to call for help in the form of law enforcement, social services, more than the usual crew of two or three, fire or a specialized rescue team such as extricators for a driver trapped in a truck.

He needs to worry about hazmat dangers, auto fires and lack of stability, domestic situations or other potentially violent scenes.

Some first responders in cities wear body armor.

Blood-borne pathogens, body substances that might be contagious, are a concern to the first responder. Books, films and television shows continue to potray medical providers casually dealing with blood, saliva and vomit. One best-selling mystery writer has her physician-character performing rescue breathing on someone with a bloody mouth without using a pocket mask! This would never happen in the real world of medicine.

The first responder, like all professional medical providers, should wear gloves while caring for a patient. Certainly when bodily fluids are present, the FR will protect his hands and don goggles, a gown or whatever might be appropriate.

The concern here is not only AIDS, which must be introduced into the body of the FR to cause a problem. Hepatitis and tuberculosis are many times more contagious and are the greatest concerns.

Contacts

The public sometimes thinks that medical providers wear gloves to protect their patient from the professional's germs. Wrong. It is the patient who is the danger and OSHA requires field medical caregivers such as first responders to protect themselves against:

HEPATITIS   Carried directly from body substances, or just by touching something that a hepatitis patient's feces, semen, food, blood or saliva has been in contact with.

HERPES   Direct contact with infected individual's broken skin or mucous membranes.

MENINGITIS   Carried through the air, by touching or through contact with anything in contact with the patient's food or mucous.

TUBERCULOSIS   Easily transmitted through the air in saliva and cough droplets.

CHAPTER FOURTEEN

Emergency Medical Technician

Above the first responder certification, the next level of EMS out-of-hospital provision of care is at the emergency medical technician or EMT level. The EMT may have taken an FR course, enjoyed the work and decided to "license up." In any event, the EMT course will cover the content of the FR course and build upon it.

The wail of a siren pierces the air signaling both "Emergency!" and "Help's coming." The EMT code is 10-8, which means it is on the way. When life hangs in the balance, an emergency crew will look to the skills possessed by this medical professional, who can make a life-and-death difference.

Yet literature, film and the media depict this EMS provider as an ambulance driver and body transporter. Constantly in books and articles, the EMT with the medic picks up dead bodies, which in reality never happens. Nowhere else in the rescue field is the public perception so incorrect. No one seems to understand what education, knowledge and skills the EMT possesses. In fact, a 1996 study showed that the public felt EMTs were doing a wonderful job, but could not describe what it is they do.

Part of the problem is that the man or woman on the street believes there is a physician in the back of the ambulance, or a nurse

---

Sign Off

The following is a typical statement the physician must sign if he wishes to be involved with the care of a patient in the field:

Non-EMS System Medical Interveners

Thank you for your offer of assistance. If you are currently providing patient care, you should be relinquishing care to these medical professionals. No individual should intervene in the care of this patient unless the individual is requested to by the attending EMT. If you feel capable of assisting, or delivering more extensive emergency medical care at the scene, the EMTs may choose to not assist you in specific deviations from their protocols. If you wish to assume responsibility for care at the scene, you must accompany the patient to the hospital.

All EMTs have dealt with the situation where a doctor insists upon taking over. When physicians are presented with intervener statements they are required to sign, their egos generally allow them to back off.

---

who is diagnosing, reading the cardiac monitor and providing care. But doctors and nurses are not trained, certified or licensed to work in the field, the prehospital setting. If a physician *insists* upon taking over from an EMT, he must sign a release taking responsibility for the patient and must agree to accompany the patient to the hospital, where he will have to explain his actions.

EMTs are used to working on the edge of the interstate, are proficient working under a flipped bus, deliver care efficiently in the dark, cramped back bedroom of a tenement apartment. They are used to improvising; they do not have assistants hovering at their elbows to hand them gear, much less eight individuals to gather around when a gunshot patient needs five procedures done at once. They do not work under the bright lights of an emergency department; they establish IVs in the mud by flashlight. This is not the familiar setting for other medical professionals. In the field and on the streets, it is the EMT who is in charge.

History of the Profession

The origin of the confusion about the prehospital provider stems from those days when the local funeral home, seemingly in a conflict of interest, also provided ambulance transport. As late as 1966, at least 50 percent of the nation's ambulance services were provided by morticians, who by now owned fleets of ambulances. Their employees, the men in white lab coats who were called ambulance attendants, arrived at the scene of an emergency, placed their patient into the white hearse and drove fast. There was no assessment, much less treatment or list of anticipated problems and solutions. In fact, no one was in the back with the patient.

That notion of load-and-go no longer exists. Today, the fully equipped ambulance with its extensively trained prehospital emergency medicine providers (referring to them as mere attendants is a throwback to earlier times when load-and-go and bag-and-drag were the bywords, rather than treat-and-stabilize) is the equivalent of the ER and its doctors and nurses. So with the exception of the patient needing surgery, what's the rush? What *is* important—and what can happen in the field that cannot in the emergency department—is that care begins within six minutes of, say, a heart attack. The exact same care the emergency department would provide.

Education and Certification

In most states, EMT courses are offered in a variety of locations. Increasingly, colleges are offering EMT courses leading to a degree in emergency medical services. Graduate degrees in EMS administration are also available. This college and graduate-level activity is relatively new. Someone evidently looked at what EMS providers were doing and realized it was equivalent to higher education knowledge and skills.

This education follows the Department of Transportation curriculum. Some states or regions within states choose to go above the DOT standard requirements and teach EMTs to do more and to know more. To find out licensing/certification requirements in a particular state or area, contact the EMS office, or this department might be under health and human services. Also, the January issues of *JEMS* (Journal of EMS, 1947 Camino Vida Roble, Suite 200, Carlsbad, CA 92008. (619) 431-9797.) lists all state offices and state EMS directors.

Many states have several levels of EMT certification, usually having to do with education, and licensure, which ties in with the privilege of practicing. Depending upon the state, the skills and knowledge an EMT might be dealing with include defibrillation, using a cardiac monitor that is the portable equivalent of what is used in a hospital, and reading, interpreting and electrically treating cardiac rhythms. EMTs decide if an IV is indicated and will establish one in the home or the rig (ambulance). They will unblock blocked airways, establish and maintain traction on a broken limb, reduce dislocations, stabilize and splint fractures, control hemorrhage and give inoculations. EMTs intubate, which means that, like the anesthesiologist in the OR, they use a tool called a laryngoscope to move aside the tongue and give a good view of the spread vocal cords. Then they slip a tube down an unconscious patient's airway to keep it open so that oxygen being blown down will not be cut off. EMTs perform phlebotomy or the drawing of bloods to save time when reaching the hospital. Respiratory therapy includes oxygen administration. When an infant needs IV fluids or access into the blood stream is necessary so the medic can inject emergency drugs, EMTs will establish an intraosseous infusion. This is the equivalent of an IV in the lower bone of a child's leg, which can be easier and safer to accomplish than attempting to hit one of his tiny veins.

For this reason, the ambulance should be written about as a mobile emergency department rather than simply a way to get the patient from the scene to the hospital whether it is an MCI or a myocardial infarction.

Qualifications

The personality type that evolves into an excellent EMT tends to enjoy being on the edge, never knowing what she might face when she arrives on-scene. Because she has no general supply to fall back on to fulfill her supply needs that might make her job easier, she is adept at improvising to use equipment and gear in ways not necessarily intended.

EMT candidates must be able to roll with the punches. In an emergency, almost definitionally, the unexpected occurs. Every case is different. In-house run reviews uncover actions not taken that

---

Support for the Patient

BASIC LIFE SUPPORT (BLS) is the stabilization of airway, breathing and circulation without specialized equipment.

ADVANCED LIFE SUPPORT (ALS) is basic life support plus definitive therapies using invasive procedures, drugs and electrical defibrillation.

---

would have made the incident less frantic. Criticism, both from self and through quality assurance (QA) sessions, will be meted out; the EMT must be able to accept imperfection and go on trying to improve.

Education is never-ending for the street emergency provider. In addition to self-study whenever a patient caused head-scratching, the EMT, unlike any other medical provider, is required to take courses as a prerequisite for license renewal. The potential EMT who thinks this is overwhelming or unimportant is not good material.

Job Description

The medical practice of all providers at every level is based upon protocols. These are a set of rules, textbook-plans that one runs down line-by-line for a specific problem. No matter the level, the medical professional, for example, will deal with those same ABCs the first responder was checking out. This includes the neurologist, the physician's assistant (PA), the certified nurse's aid (CNA) and the EMT.

The difference that the EMT deals with as she assesses the patient, identifies problems and plans treatment, is her mobile environment.

A 911 call comes in and the EMT is on her way. In big cities, EMTs are usually on an ambulance with a medic partner. In more rural settings, two or three EMTs might respond, calling for para-medic backup if advanced skills are required. All will attend to their patient as a crew at the scene; one will drive. Frequently, crew members take turns, assuming primary responsibility for patient care every second or third run.

Before their shift started—and EMS coverage is generally provided twenty-four hours a day, seven days a week, including all holidays—the crew completed an ambulance inventory. All of the tools and supplies the first responder has in her jump kit are on the ambulance, along with bulkier, more delicate instrumentation. Everything must be in-date and in working order before each shift.

In the field, as the patient is being evaluated, an EMT will go out to the rig to get whatever might be needed that is not in the jump kits. The FR has reported on the patient's vitals—pulse, blood pressure, respirations—completing the medical providers' first job of: checking the airway, breathing and circulation, the ABCs of life support.

Notes continue to be taken as more information is gathered. While her partners talk with the patient and his family members, a third EMT might hook up oxygen and place a nonrebreather mask over the patient's nose and mouth. This mask, combined with high-flow oxygen, ensures that every breath receives nearly 100 percent oxygen, and oxygen, known as "Os," is one of the best drugs available for any ailment. The EMT gathers medical history as an indicator of what might be happening again. Any medications? Allergies? There is a litany of questions and examinations that the EMT goes through that forms the basis for a patient history (H_x), the history of present illness (HPI), physical exam (PE), chief complaint (C/C), diagnosis (D_x) and treatment (T_x). Mentally, the EMT will create a problem plan: If what is being done does not produce the desired effect or if new issues arise, how will she deal with this new set of circumstances?

The medical role of the EMT is to stabilize, reaching the point where the patient will not go downhill between the ambulance response and delivery to the hospital. Once the crew is comfortable that their patient is stable, the team together goes about the business of preparing the patient for transport.

"Packaging the patient," getting him ready for the ambulance ride, usually is a matter of moving him carefully to a rolling stretcher (called a cot), covering him as appropriate with sheets and blankets, and then strapping him in so there is no danger of an unexpected fall. Once in the rig, the cot is clicked into several fastening devices so that it doesn't roll around while the ambulance is underway.

If the patient has suffered trauma and there is any worry about neurological damage to the spinal chord, packaging begins with carefully strapping the patient to a long board so that he is immobilized. Then a combination of foam blocks and tape is used to hold his head stationary. Once the EMTs are sure that no careless spinal movement can compound the injuries that are already present, the immobilized patient will be moved to the cot and the ambulance.

The most common style of ambulance consists of a "box" mounted on a truck chassis. The ride in the back of this vehicle can be rocky. Most EMTs are too tall to be able to stand straight, so they hunch over their patient or sit on the long bench lining one side of the rig. Procedures requiring a delicate hand such as establishing an intravenous line can be tough. If the patient is a difficult "stick," the driver might be asked to pull over during the five-second procedure, or the EMT might access the vein while the ambulance idles at a red light.

There are times when the EMTs are thrown about as the ambulance winds through traffic. For provider safety, there are padded headliners along the walls and handrails on the ceiling, which double as equipment stands. Like sailors, the providers develop rig-legs and get used to keeping their balance while performing all sorts of procedures. EMTs have been known to sprawl across patients in particularly difficult driving situations.

Because the ambulance, an EMT's office, is disinfected after each run, it has that usual antiseptic hospital smell. Rigs are air-conditioned; the driver might have a radio and tape deck, which are played when the patient is not being transported. Sometimes, when the patient is nonemergent, soft music might be soothing for everybody's frazzled nerves.

Supplies are stowed in clear, glass-fronted cabinets, often affixed with large identifying numbers that correspond with an inventory list. (See a typical inventory list later in this chapter.)

Stabilizing the patient is the EMT's top priority. When time and responsibilities permit, the EMT must fill out and sign a call or run sheet that will be left at the emergency department and inserted into the patient's permanent hospital record. Physicians and nurses will refer to this run sheet to better understand the patient's baseline and presenting condition.

RUN REPORT #	Mo.	Day	Year	M T W Th	F S Sun	SERVICE NAME		SERVICE NO.	VEHICLE NO.	ALS ☐ Performed ☐ Back-up Called	SERVICE RUN NO.

421301

NAME — BILLING INFORMATION

STREET OR R.F.D.

CITY/TOWN — STATE — ZIP

AGE / DATE OF BIRTH ☐ Male ☐ Female — PHONE

INCIDENT LOCATION: ADDRESS — SITE CODE — CITY/TOWN

TRANSPORTED TO: — TREATING / FAMILY PHYSICIAN — CREW LICENSE NUMBERS

TRANSPORTATION / COMMUNICATIONS PROBLEMS

☐ Medical
☐ Cardiac
☐ Poisoning/OD
☐ Respiratory
☐ Behavioral
☐ Diabetic
☐ Seizure
☐ CVA
☐ OB/GYN
☐ Other _____
☐ Cardiac Arrest/ Code 99

☐ Trauma
☐ Multi-Systems Trauma
☐ Head
☐ Spinal
☐ Burn
☐ Soft Tissue Injury
☐ Fractures
☐ Other _____

☐ MEDICATIONS

CHIEF COMPLAINT:

☐ AOB / ETOH
☐ MVA
Restraints:
Seatbelts ☐ Used ☐ Not Used ☐ N/A
☐ Helmet
☐ Childseat
☐ Airbag

☐ ALLERGIES

R	L	Lung Sounds
☐	☐	Clear
☐	☐	Absent
☐	☐	Decreased
☐	☐	Rales
☐	☐	Wheeze
☐	☐	Stridor

TYPE OF RUN
☐ Emergency Transport
☐ Routine Transfer
☐ Emergency Transfer
☐ No Transport
☐ Refused Transport

TIME	CODE	ODOMETER
Call Received		
Enroute		
At Scene		
From Scene		
At Destination		
In Service		

TIME	PULSE	RESP	BP	PUPILLARY RESPONSE	SKIN	EYE OPENING RESPONSE	VERBAL RESPONSE	MOTOR RESPONSE	CAPILLARY REFILL
						4 3 2 1	5 4 3 2 1	6 5 4 3 2 1	☐ Normal ☐ Delayed ☐ None
						4 3 2 1	5 4 3 2 1	6 5 4 3 2 1	☐ Normal ☐ Delayed ☐ None
						4 3 2 1	5 4 3 2 1	6 5 4 3 2 1	☐ Normal ☐ Delayed ☐ None

MUTUAL AID:
Assisted/Assisted by Service # _____ Time Called: _____

PATIENT'S SUSPECTED PROBLEM: **421301**

Cleared Airway	Extrication
Artificial Respiration/BVM	Cervical Immobilization
Oropharyngeal Airway	KED/Short Board
Nasopharyngeal Airway	Long Board
CPR–Time:	Restraints
Bystander CPR	Traction Splinting
AED	General Splinting
Suction	Cold Application
Oxygen–LP Min___ ☐ Nasal ☐ Mask	MAST Inflated
Pulse Oximetry	
Autovent	

☐ Medication Administered
☐ Monitor
☐ Pacing

EOA
☐ SUC LIC. # _____
☐ UNSUC LIC. # _____

LIC # | EKG RHYTHM | TIME | MEDS / DEFIB / C-VERT | DOSE W/S | ROUTE

☐ Defib C-Vert ☐
Lic # _____
☐ Chest Decomp
☐ Cricothyrotomy

MEDICAL CONTROL ☐ Written Order/Protocol ☐ Verbal Order/Protocol

IV ☐ SUC LIC. # _____ Total Attempts
☐ UNSUC LIC. # _____

ET ☐ SUC LIC. # _____ Total Attempts
☐ UNSUC LIC. # _____

NAME OF E.D. TREATING PHYSICIAN — SIGNATURE OF CREW MEMBER IN CHARGE — COPY 1 HOSPITAL

1/95

421301 | Month | Day | Year | **EMERGENCY DEPARTMENT REPORT** | Name of Hospital

(1) ☐ Medical (2) ☐ Cardiac (3) ☐ Poisoning/OD (4) ☐ Respiratory (5) ☐ Behavioral (6) ☐ Diabetic (7) ☐ Seizure (8) ☐ CVA (9) ☐ OB/Gyn (10) ☐ Other ___ (11) ☐ Cardiac Arrest/Code 99
(12) ☐ Trauma (13) ☐ Multi-Systems Trauma (14) ☐ Head (15) ☐ Spinal (16) ☐ Burn (17) ☐ Soft Tissue Injury (18) ☐ Fractures (19) ☐ Other _____

TIME	PULSE	RESP	BP	PUPILLARY RESPONSE	SKIN	EYE OPENING RESPONSE	VERBAL RESPONSE	MOTOR RESPONSE	CAPILLARY REFILL
						4 3 2 1	5 4 3 2 1	6 5 4 3 2 1	(1) ☐ Normal (2) ☐ Delayed (3) ☐ None

E. D. Record # — Patient I. D. #

TREATMENT: (1) ☐ None (2) ☐ Medical (3) ☐ Surgical (4) ☐ Psychiatric (5) ☐ Other

Patient Disposition — Indications for Transfer (As Stated in Protocol)

DISCHARGED: (1) ☐ Nursing Home (2) ☐ Home (3) ☐ AMA (4) ☐ Rehab (5) ☐ Other
HOSPITALIZED: (6) ☐ ICU/CCU (7) ☐ General
DIED: (8) ☐
TRANSFERRED TO: (9) ☐ ECF/SNF (10) ☐ Hospital _____ Date _____ Time _____

A typical run sheet which is completed by EMS providers. A narrative describing the incident and the care rendered would appear on the reverse. One copy is left at the hospital for reference in the emergency department, while the carbon copies go back in the ambulance to be used for billing, quality assurance, statistical studies and education. The emergency department copy becomes the back page of the patient's permanent hospital record. Note the tear-off stub at the bottom, to be completed by the emergency department and filed by the hospital.

> ### *Star of Life*
>
> As you describe your ambulance, comment on its lights and sirens and the fact that the word AMBULANCE is written in reverse so that it can be read in the rearview mirror of the car ahead. Also mention the prominent star of life, usually blue. It is a six-barred cross, the symbol of EMS. The staff in the center represents medicine and healing.

At the hospital, the EMT will turn over patient care by giving a report to the receiving party: an emergency physician, PA or nurse. This is routine for all medical personnel as they transfer care. The EMT will have information no one else can possess for she was at the scene. As she presents the case's C/C, HPI, and PE-findings, she is aware that she is the eyes and ears of the doctor in terms of conveying the mechanism of injury (MOI). For example, the EMT will describe the damage done to a car, indicative of the particular trauma the doctor can then be on the lookout for. The EMT might correct the version on whether the child really did fall down the stairs or was pushed—the EMT saw the stairs, and spoke with the grandmother and the neighbor who came running.

The EMT can convey why the patient is complaining of the mother-of-all-headaches because the EMT saw the spidered windshield that the patient's head impacted on. The medical professional knows the elderly patient's altered sensorium in the form of lack of response might have to do with improper nourishment because the refrigerator had no food in it. The rescuer reports the patient was noncompliant with his meds because the responder spotted them by the bedside with the cotton plugs intact.

As the EMT delivers her patient, she might assure him that the cat was left with the neighbor and the front door was locked. Because it is the EMT who is there at the scene, a special bond develops. An emergency is a problem that cannot be handled, where help is needed to prevent serious illness or death. The patient was relieved to hear that the EMTs had arrived and to finally be in their competent hands. Often dangerously high blood pressure readings will dive to acceptable levels within minutes of the EMTs' arrival; unbearable pain is often relieved simply when an EMT wipes the sweat off a wet forehead.

Language

Medical providers follow the same protocols that identify the most consistently successful diagnostic plan and treatment for the particular problem. It is the medical communities' cookbook method of delivering medical care, and it is practiced throughout the world.

EMTs who maintain that same standard of care stabilize according to their EMS protocols. These are the same for EMTs throughout the country.

A Tennessee EMT vacationing in Alaska comes upon a 10-55, a motor vehicle accident (MVA). She goes over to the unconscious driver, and as she tick-tocks through the ABCs, she stabilizes the spine to protect it against further injury. A responding ambulance pulls up and two EMTs jump out. One takes C-spine mobilization from the Tennessee EMT, so she can slip a hard plastic collar around the victim's neck. Then she pulls traction on an open femur fracture, so the other Alaska EMT applies a traction splint. The three work side-by-side having never met before and certainly never worked together.

This is a true-life occurrence that tends to bind together the nation's EMTs. The cowboy aspect of riding to the scene of trouble and, through aggressive treatments, making things better for the victims tends to appeal to a certain sort of personality. These self-sufficient type-A personalities feel connected to each other throughout the country.

By its nature, EMS is about unfortunate events. The in-language of prehospital EMS across America lightens the load as the clubby EMTs chat with one another about cases and treatments. Your EMT-character will call her ambulance a "rig" or "truck" and the working end of it will be referred to as "the box." Patients within the rig sometimes UAD, up-and-die, and when no one knows why, the answer is " 'cause." Some elderly patients suffer from OTH or over-the-hill. Oxygen might be called Os, as in "Give him some Os, stat."

Sometimes "a little tincture of time" helps the patient. EMTs "beat feet" to get to a patient who is about to "crash and burn." This is a case where the responders would not have decided to "Stay and play," but to "Load and go."

EMTs know "All bleeding stops," and that, eventually, "All patients die." They know that "All of us are dying of a disease; it's called mortality."

Although the goal of the EMT is to stabilize, there are times when a patient is FTD, or "fixin' to die," and the only treatment is to "drive fast."

Dangers

Emergency responders have an occupational hazard connected to the way they live, the fast foods they eat.

If an EMT is on duty, she is on. No one spells her so that she can go to dinner. She and her partner take the ambulance and head for the local food establishment that provides takeout; if the crew tries to sit down and eat, their dispatcher is sure to call them out. Better to have the food packaged to move, then sit there in the restaurant and eat it. Or eat in the cab of her rig, parked by a curb. Or skip meals and live on coffee as calls keep coming and coming, throughout the shift.

In recognition of the lifestyle of the EMT, someone once said that, prior to the invention of coffee, there was no EMS.

In addition to digestive ills, EMTs are known for their aching backs. They lift patients, carry them down stairs, up out of boat holds, up road embankments, vertically within small elevators, up and down and under grandstands. There's an EMT line that says, "The sicker they are, the higher they climb." This relates to ill people feeling they must crawl to the third floor before collapsing.

A trick EMTs try to remember to save their backs is to stare into your partner's eyes as the cot is lifted. It encourages lifting with the knees, keeping the back straight.

Nonetheless, it is not unusual to find an EMT with an aching back, cooling her heels on the cot in the back of the idle ambulance as it waits in the bay, always ready for the next run.

Equipment

The following list is of the contents of a typical ambulance:

INTERIOR

Cab

2 flashlights
binoculars
hazmat guide
locator book
clipboard
pen
2 driver's oxygen forms
6 mileage stubs
ferry tickets
slot screw driver
registration
change purse
pen
pencil
fire extinguisher

Action Area

IV equipment
AED
sharps box
glucometer
pad/pencils
reference pads
oral thermometer
suction

#1

portable suction
hand-held suction
drug box
burn kit
bag valve mask—infant/ped

BP cuffs, 5 sizes
ALS A/W kit/intubation gear
    including laryngoscope and
    blades
ALS surgical A/W
drug box journal
jump kit

#2

N/S irrigation
sterile water/irrigation
OB kits (2)

#3

normal saline IV solution (check
    date)
ringer's IV solution (check date)
D5W IV solution (check date)
3 IV blue bags w/macro set ups
thermo IV bag

Rear Wall

2 O_2 cylinders
1 O_2 cylinder w/NiO_2 mixing
    valve

#4

gauze pads/4 × 4; 3 × 3; 2 × 2
trauma pad
2 giant trauma dressings
assorted Band-Aids
6 × 6 trauma pads
tape
6 Kling

2 elastic bandages
4 triangular bandages

Under Bench
oxygen wrenches
traction splint
O₂ main cylinder
5 ladder splints
2 SAM splints
3 large rigid splints
broom
mop
sign
Teflon pipe tape

On Bench
stethoscope
BP cuff
1 heavy blanket
bag valve mask

Monitor Counter
cardiac monitor
basket: BSI hand wipes
BP cuff in basket
stethoscope
small gloves
EMT scissors
bandage scissors
IV infuser (hanging)
Kelly clamp
oral A/W kit
tissues
ACLS chart
PALS chart

#5
8 glycerine swabs

3 activated charcoal (check date)
2 glucose tubes (check date)
emesis basin
2 vomitus bags
teddy bear
set wrist restraints
3 BSI isolation kits

#6
4 foil blankets
2 SAM splints
2 burn sheets
4 small rigid splints

#7
urinal
bed pan
3 bath blankets
6 hand towels
4 Chux pads
2 johnnies
4 sheets
2 pillowcases
3 washcloths
1 pillow

Cot
1 hand towel
run book
1 heavy blanket
1 bath blanket
1 pillow
pulse oximeter

Under Seat
3 isolation kits
10 run sheets

#8
White resuscitator
2 infant nonrebreather masks
2 pedi nonrebreather masks
3 adult nonrebreather masks
3 nasal cannulas
2 pkgs. oxygen tubing
2 nebulizers
2 disposable
   humidifier-bottles
box oral A/W
2 disposable suction bags
2 suction catheters 16 fr; 14 fr
6 nasal A/W—8.0; 8.5; 8.7;
   9.4; 10.0; 10.8
2 Yankauer tips
1 pocket mask

#9
6 goggles, protective
surgical mask box
box large gloves
box medium gloves
box small gloves

#10
3 BSI spill kits
6 biohazard bags

#11
ambulance disinfectant
4 ziplock bags
boxes of trash bags—
   2 sizes
Saran Wrap
aluminum foil
cleaning gloves
disinfectant towelettes

Locked Cabinet
nitrous oxide

EXTERIOR
Passenger-side/Rear
tarp
inflatable splints
infant car seat
toddler car seat
Back/Right
broom
mop
cleaning supplies
splints
umbrella
Hare splint

Back/Left
evacu-splint/pump
BSI green box
vacuum splint/pump

Driver-side/Rear
chocks
tools
rope
come-along
flares
triangles
gray medical tape

Driver-side/Cntr.
stair chair
hard hats
MAST
cold water survival suits
traffic vests

rain suit
MCI kit
light sticks
lug wrench

Driver-side/Front
Stiff Neck collars
Philly collars
KED

Sager splint
Halloween splints
scoop stretcher
backboard
spider straps
head blocks
backboard
yellow straps

Those Who Treat

CHAPTER FIFTEEN

Paramedic

During a heart attack, time equals heart muscle that will survive the event. During a stroke, time equals viable brain tissue. When a diabetic crashes because he has miscalculated his insulin dosage, time is also of the essence. Medical and trauma crises don't wait upon transportation to a distant emergency room, they demand action now.

That action is the paramedic.

Arriving on-scene in a thoroughly equipped ALS ambulance, the medic brings an emergency room to the accident. He can perform numerous lifesaving procedures and does them in the patient's bedroom, on the side of the road or in the back of a pretzled automobile. His medical world is not as sterile or organized as an emergency department, but he can get the job done. The most common media misconception of paramedic practice ignores this fact.

Authors and screenwriters consistently show the medic in a bag-and-drag mode, scooping up a patient and driving fast to the hospital. An extension of this observation is that lifesaving medical procedures *per force* are delayed until the patient reaches the hospital. This is wrong. If definitive medical care as delayed until the hospital was reached, nationally our statistics for surviving major events such as car accidents and heart attacks would be much more dismal.

Consider that the gold standard of emergency care, on the streets as well as in the hospital, is based upon the ABCs or airway, breathing and circulation. If these three life processes can be maintained and stabilized, then the patient stands a good chance of surviving the event intact, without permanent brain, heart or other vital organ damage. At a minimum, medics insert a variety of tubes into the throat and larynx, artificially keeping an airway open. They know how to remove developing pressures in the chest cavity so that the lungs can inflate and breathing can continue. They use drugs to drive overwhelming fluids out of the lungs, making space for oxygen absorption. Finally, medics have in their jump kits and ambulance a variety of chemical and electrical therapies that control or restore heart rhythms so that blood oxygenated by the lungs can be pumped by the heart throughout the body. All of these activities amount to saving tissue and saving lives, which is what being a paramedic is all about.

The pay of paramedics, which is usually an hourly wage with benefits and overtime at time-and-a-half, is not commensurate with their knowledge and responsibility for human lives. The men and women who make paramedicine a career do so because they love it. If they need to work sixty-hour weeks on the ambulance or carry a second job in order to make ends meet, so be it. On top of these busy schedules, many medics will volunteer their services in the communities where they live, picking up one or two runs a week in their time off.

While street medicine is exciting and intellectually stimulating, it also can be very physically and emotionally draining. For this reason, medics burn out early and often, and the practice is a young person's game. Older medics in their forties drift into increased teaching and training responsibilities, producing the next generation of field practitioners. Alternatively, they become administrators in the larger ambulance services, supervising, training and making sure that their service continues to provide quality, state-of-the-art pre-hospital medicine.

History of the Profession

By 1966, when the "Accidental Death and Disability" White Paper was issued by the National Research Council, the principles of speed in the practice of emergency medicine and providing care in the field were already well-established. A hospital-based "ambulance surgeon" was working on the streets of Manhattan in 1903. The U.S. military had long since developed the principles of medevac medicine, using helicopters to transport the wounded to field hospitals. Riding on those helicopters were corpsmen or, later, medics who provided lifesaving care before their patients got to the MASH units so familiar to TV viewers. In Belfast, Ireland, the Royal Victoria Hospital was running Flying Squad, which was the first out-of-hospital cardiac care unit.

The paramedic as an EMS license level was born in 1967, spawned by all of these precedents and nursed by the nation's growing concern with the principles of emergency cardiac care as enumerated by the AHA and the Red Cross. Pittsburgh began providing advanced level care in 1966 by training inner-city providers and staffing ambulances with a physician. The first formal training programs for paramedics began in Pittsburgh, Miami and Baltimore in the late 1960s.

By 1971, the Columbus, Ohio, fire department put onto city streets the first prehospital coronary care unit manned by "squad men" without the presence of a physician. The principle of medics working calls by themselves without the direct, on-scene involvement of physicians was born. To this day, however, most advanced EMS practices are still under the theoretical supervision of a physician, listening in to the call at a radio in the emergency department. This supervision is called on-line medical control, though rarely does it exist in anything other than name alone. It is how doctors, convinced of the benefits of rapid medical responses, were persuaded to relinquish to paramedics direct control of "their" medical procedures, and it is an underlying rationale for medics' continually expanding scope of practice.

Also in 1971, Johnny and Roy, the paramedic stars of TV's *Emergency*, hit the streets of Los Angeles and the televisions of millions of households across the nation. Their skills, derring-do and employment as fire station medics influenced an entire generation of adolescents. To this day, Johnny and Roy remain cult figures in the world of emergency medicine. Their exploits, while overly dramatized, are still more accurate media representations of the practice of paramedicine than anything that has come along since.

The first formal paramedic curriculum was formatted by the Department of Transportation in 1975. It was a consensus document, representing the best thinking of physicians, EMS providers and medical researchers, but it included training and testing in some accessing and all of the stabilizing skills as well as a full complement of field-treatment skills. It also required extensive internships and experiences in a variety of hospital departments and on busy ambulances working under the direct supervision of experienced medics. This curriculum was rewritten in 1996–1997 to reflect changes in practice and to bring the practice of paramedicine to the threshold of the twenty-first century.

Education and Certification

Paramedic programs throughout the country, whether sponsored by a state, EMS region or college or university, include hospital rotations in coronary care, psychology, surgery, anesthesia, burn unit, pediatrics, respiratory therapy, phlebotomy, intensive care and obstetrics.

In addition to all first responder and EMT skills and education, the medic learns to perform chest decompression, transtracheal jet insufflation and surgical cricothyrotomy. He will have mastered the identification and treatment of up to twenty different cardiac rhythms that can be treated and/or reversed by electrical and chemical therapies.

Didactic education in the specialty is equivalent in hours to two years post-graduate work.

Unlike other medical professionals, like doctors and nurses who are licensed forever, paramedics must show competence and relicense every few years, depending upon their state's requirements. A demonstration of continuing proficiency and knowledge is the requirement for CME credits in areas like pharmacology, basic medical, advanced cardiac and trauma.

Qualifications

A medic is licensed to perform at and beyond the BLS level. He will be asked to deliver advanced cardiac life support (ACLS), usually a required certification for medics that the majority of other medical professionals (with the exception of cardiologists and emergency physicians) do not possess. Like every other provider in the world, they focus upon the medical ABCs plus D, for drugs or therapies such as drug infusion. Paramedics are ready to assess any emergency and practice at a level as diverse as hand-holding and thoracenteses, which is the surgical removal of fluids from the chest cavity.

Job Description

The ultimate display of the paramedic's skill and knowledge is running what is called a code, which is a series of procedures performed when it is sensible and medically feasible to think about trying to restart the heart of someone who has died.

Here's how it works: White-water rescuers pulled a young subject from the raging river, and a wilderness first responder found the victim to be breathless and pulseless.

CPR is in progress as the medic arrives with his portable electrocardiogram (ECG). (They're not too far off the road, so it was carried in.) He sees good CPR being performed—the chest is rising with each compression. Good.

He hooks up his ECG to the patient; three wires leading from the machine have round, paperlike patches at the ends. One of the patches is attached to the front of each shoulder; the third goes on the left hip.

Then the medic takes a look at the ECG screen and sees a rhythm called ventricular fibrillation. This rhythm is a squiggly line because the heart is wiggling but doing nothing useful for its body, which is now starving for oxygenation.

The victim is young; her heart had nothing wrong with it before she took in too much water. CPR was begun within a couple of minutes of her drowning. This is the setting where there is a chance that the medic might be able to bring her back if he does everything right.

In a few seconds, a light goes on indicating his paddles are charged. He places them on his young patient, one on each side of the heart. "Stand back," he calls out. "Everyone back." Then, after he looks to be sure no one is touching the patient, he depresses the SHOCK buttons on each paddle.

The patient's body jerks in response to the shock. He checks the ECG. Still V-fib. Immediately he recharges the paddles but turns up the electricity a notch and shocks again.

"Start CPR."

CPR is performed on the dead, those who have no heartbeat, which is what the pulse is, and are not breathing.

But how does the first person on-scene know whether to start CPR—whether the victim is breathing or not? After opening the mouth and tilting the head back, she should look, listen and feel for breathing. *Look* for the chest to rise. *Listen* with her ear close to the subject's mouth. *Feel* by placing her cheek close to the victim's mouth. If there is no breath, the rescuer will give two breaths, exhaling twice into the victim's mouth, and go on to establish if the nonbreathing victim still has a beating heart.

Then she will place her fingertips on the subject's carotid artery, located on both sides of the neck, under the chin at about Adam's apple level, then halfway back toward the ear.

If there is a pulse, she will need to continue to rescue breathe for the victim. By now, hopefully, someone will have gone/called/radioed for a medic.

In the meantime, the victim's pumping heart is distributing the oxygen the person is delivering by continuing to rescue breathe.

If there is no breath and no pulse, start CPR. That's the rule and it's real simple. No breath, no pulse? Start CPR. Rescuers say it over and over as they practice proper CPR techniques.

CPR is a combination of rescue breathing and chest compressions. The oxygen is blown in and then the compressions are started, done atop the breastbone, called the sternum, to pump it around the body.

No change. He recharges.

In the meantime, his crew of two EMTs have arrived with the ambulance. He orders one to get ready to intubate, which involves slipping a plastic tube down the throat of the patient so that oxygen from a tank the EMTs brought over can have a straight shot down to the lungs.

After a third defibrillation at the highest level he can use, his EMTs have intubated. As one prepares to establish IV access so the medic will have a route into the bloodstream to push drugs, the other is squeezing the balloonlike end of a special bellowslike bag valve mask. This pumps oxygen down that endotracheal tube now sticking out the patient's mouth and taped to her face.

The medic will work down an established ACLS protocol or treatment for V-fib, the same one every emergency provider, including doctors and nurses in emergency departments, follows. He will administer through the IV port a concentration of adrenalin, called epinephrine. Then he will shock, hoping the epi will make the heart more sensitive to the electrical therapy.

Still not successful? Next he tries a different drug, lidocaine. Shock. Then bretylium. Shock. Procainamide. Shock.

He's worked his way pretty far down the algorhythm by now. And he is worried that he has lost this young patient when he again checks his ECG and sees the rhythm change!

He will have to respond pharmacologically as various rhythms shoot across his screen. The heart is still a bit shaky. But once V-fib is behind them, he begins to hope that he has a save.

The patient does not sit up, say, "Where am I?" and walk away. Although this has happened, it is rare. In fact, this near-drowning victim's heart will go through several dangerous rhythms as the medic might try to stabilize the irritable heart with an IV drip containing the drug lidocaine, a calming medication. Then this patient will spend a few days in the hospital's cardiac intensive care unit. Such cases have been known to revert, even days later.

Usually when a code is run, the surrounding area looks like a disaster area. Every second counts. The longer it takes to bring a patient back, the more chance that irreversible damage has been done. So medication boxes have been ripped open and flung away. IV gear is thrown here and there. Everyone involved is exhausted.

And happy. Tentatively. It looks good. They did it.

Equipment

The EMS provider who can push drugs, which is idiomatic for administering drug through a special IV line-port, is the medic. The paramedic you write into your tale has great possibilities to save lives or, if he makes a mistake, to kill people. This is because all his medicines are designed to deal with life-threatening medical problems, to turn them around. If he mistakenly decides a heart is beating too fast and pushes lidocaine to slow it down, the resulting seriously slowed or stopped heart will be a problem.

Usually those handling such potent drugs work in a hospital and have others looking over their shoulders. In the emergency department, there is a chart on the wall detailing the use of those drugs the medic carries, along with appropriate dosage.

Out there in the snowstorm with the downed hunter in the middle of a heart attack, the medic needs to remember what he should be doing and when.

The equipment he is carrying in a drug box will typically include all those cardiac drugs he used during a code in the "Job Description" section: adenosine, atropine, dopamine, epinephrine, lidocaine, sodium bicarbonate, thiamine, plus:

ALBUTEROL For breathing difficulties, referred to as SOB, or shortness of breath, resulting from allergies, asthma or bronchitis.

AMINOPHYLLINE Used to reduce the swelling in connection with asthma, pulmonary edema (swelling of lung tissue) and other SOB illnesses.

ASPIRIN Used for patients whose heart has a clotting problem about to cause or causing a heart attack. An early aspirin makes clot-blocking medicines, called thrombolytics, more effective.

CHARCOAL A liquid given to overdosing patients, it absorbs the poisonous material in the belly so it does not enter the whole system.

CYANIDE ANTIDOTE Reverses the effects of the deadly gaseous compound.

DEXTROSE Administered to diabetics who took their insulin but did not ingest enough food.

DIAZEPAM Is commonly known by the trade name, Valium. It is used to calm patients, diminish pain from procedures and terminate seizures.

DIPHENHYDRAMINE Is commonly known by the trade name Benadryl. It is used for life-threatening allergic reactions with signs throughout the body, or systemically.

FUROSEMIDE Is commonly known by the trade name Lasix. It drives excess fluids from the body. This diuretic deals with a flood in the respiratory system that is causing SOB, and, finally, respiratory arrest.

GLUCAGON Encourages processes needed to make sugar available to a diabetic's body.

MEPERIDINE Is commonly known by the trade name Demerol. It is morphine produced in a test tube and is used to reduce pain for those allergic to morphine. Demerol is given to certain cardiac patients because it makes it easier for the heart to pump.

MORPHINE A narcotic used to reduce pain, and it reduces the force needed by the heart to pump blood.

NALOXONE Naloxone is commonly known by the trade name Narcan. It reverses the effects of narcotics and will also bring newborns with respiratory difficulties back to life and will stop seizures.

NITROGLYCERINE NG stops the heart pain called angina by reducing the heart's need for oxygen, which is why the patient had angina in the first place.

NITROUS OXIDE Laughing gas is used for pain management.

PROMETHAZINE Is commonly known by the trade name Phenergan. It helps nauseous patients; it is an antihistamine that reduces the effects of an allergic reaction. This drug will be given in conjunction with, for example, Demerol, so the medic will not have to record on her run sheet (N/V), which stands for nausea and vomiting.

Language

A hardworking medic deals with trauma and all sorts of medical problems from epilepsy to strokes to diabetes to abdominal emergencies. But the language he speaks fluently and frequently, and the place where his presence most consistently saves life, is when there is a cardiac emergency.

When the medic arrives in his response vehicle, an ill patient has been checked out and stabilized by an FR and EMT. He will bring with him the tools of his trade in his jump kit, which will include the instruments needed to do the special lifesaving procedures he is trained to perform. In his other hand will be a cardiac monitor, called an electrocardiogram or EKG (the K is from the German), or ECG.

In addition to defibrillating a patient, this dual tool will take a read on the sickly soul's heart. The medic watches the screen for a bit and will then make a print, called a strip, of the rhythm of the heart.

Aside from rhythms, the ECG gives the same information as the taking of a pulse. Pulse readings are the rate of the heartbeat, which can be read off the ECG or felt wherever an artery—a vessel carrying blood from the heart to the body's organs—stretches over a bone.

If the patient is feeling fine and has a normal, healthy heart, his heartbeat will be between sixty and one hundred beats a minute. If he is suffering with a heart that is beating too slowly, his pulse will be below sixty.

When a heart beats below sixty beats per minute (bradycardia) or more than one hundred beats per minute (tachycardia), the pre-hospital medical provider will see a slowed down or speeded up rhythm. If a part of the four-chambered heart is not filling or emptying effectively, the trained ECG expert will see that. Different locations within the heart have different tasks; if things are not going the way they should, the medic will be able to recognize and hopefully treat the problem and know what to do about it. There are times when medics, like all medical pros, have to recognize that some medical conditions are not treatable. Here are a few of the dozens of rhythms he might see:

ASYSTOLE This is the famous flat line. The heart is still. This is an ominous sign; to bring someone back from asystole is a long shot.

NORMAL SINUS RHYTHM (NSR) The heart is beating between 60 and 100; the QRS wave, that triangular blip along the line, looks great. It is narrow, not wide and all of the QRS complexes look alike. Everything is in sync and on time as blood in need of oxygen enters the heart, gets turfed to the lungs to pick up oxygen, then gets pumped back into the heart to be shoved out into the whole body.

PULSELESS ELECTRICAL ACTIVITY (PEA) As you can see, this looks fine, like NSR, except that the patient looks dead. What's going on? Here's where the famous admonition, "Treat the patient, not the rhythm," comes into play. The heart's electrical activity is working just dandy; the heart is getting its charge and should be bleeping along. But it's not. It is dead. PEA can be the result of a variety of problems. The fact is, unless the medic can figure out what is causing it and can make that problem go away, he's lost his patient.

Asystole.

Normal Sinus Rhythm (NSR).

Pulseless Electrical Activity (PEA)

Sinus Bradycardia (Sinus Brady)

Sinus Tachycardia (Sinus Tach)

Ventricular Fibrillation (V-Fib)

Ventricular Tachycardia (V-Tach)

SINUS BRADYCARDIA (SINUS BRADY) The pump is working too slowly. The medic can see the QRS wave is less frequent than it is on the NSR strip, mentioned earlier.

SINUS TACHYCARDIA (SINUS TACH) The opposite of sinus brady. This ticker is bopping along too fast. The patient will feel breathless and weak as the heart, in its insistence to pump, doesn't wait for the volume of blood to be present before it moves it along. The medic will give the patient a good dosing of oxygen (high-flow oxygen using a nonrebreather mask). The paramedic needs to figure out what is causing the sinus tach and how to slow things down.

VENTRICULAR FIBRILLATION (V-FIB) A heart in V-fib is so disorganized that it is not pumping at all. It is a dead heart, and the body is soon to follow. This rhythm is worked as a code. See the section under "Job Description."

VENTRICULAR TACHYCARDIA (V-TACH) This heart is beating too fast and is a bit more serious than the one with sinus tach. Here, the heart chambers responsible for the serious pumping, the ventricles, aren't working up to par. The medic will pay close attention because this rhythm, if not checked, tends to deteriorate into V-fib and a code.

When a V-tach rhythm is present and there is no pulse beat, it is akin to V-fib; your paramedic will react with full ACLS V-fib protocols. In a witnesses arrest—a professional responder saw the victim go into this rhythm—the medic treats with electrical (defibrillation) and chemical (drugs to enhance the defibrillation's effect), providing a chance to bring back the patient. Not a big chance, but a hope. And if it happens, the medic will experience the high that goes along with saving a life.

But the patient might be one of those whose last beat of his heart should be the last beat of his heart. While the near-drowning child's heart is too good to die, some hearts are too sick to live. This is the situation where the medic will be holding a hand rather than a paddle to the chest.

A common mistake storytellers make is that they have nonbreathing people down with no pulse for twenty minutes before CPR is started and before a medic initiates treatment. Keep in mind that the rapid restoration, six to ten minutes, of a beating heart remains the best way to restart a thinking brain.

So, if there is not CPR in progress within fifteen minutes of a patient's flip into V-fib or asystole, it is best not to initiate it because the patient will be "gorked," the medical in-term for a body without a thinking brain.

Dangers

Driven partly by economics and partly because they care, paramedics work long hours in a variety of contexts. On an eight-, twelve- or twenty-four-hour day, there's no telling what a busy medic will run into. Imagine twelve, twenty, thirty times a day just dropping whatever you're doing and rushing off into the unknown.

Dispatch will try to get enough information from the 911 caller to tell you what to expect, but frequently the call is garbled, the informant hysterical. This means that you and your crew are on your own. Every run is a new adventure, a new rush of anticipation and excitement. This up-and-down nature of the job breeds emotional exhaustion and frazzled nerves.

EMS as a system practices critical incident stress debriefing (CISD), which is meant to defuse the traumatic calls. Group counseling sessions give everyone at a particularly nasty call a chance to vent, to express their emotions and to learn to live with the horrors recently experienced. But CISD doesn't deal with the day-to-day grind and the accumulation of little horrors. Worse, CISD doesn't have a way to counteract the accretion of numbness and blindness. Once you have "seen it all," and it doesn't take a medic long to get to that point, every new example of horror is desensitized and remote. It becomes easier to close down, to do your job and go home without processing what is going on before your eyes.

This progression that leads to getting used to horrible things is the ultimate danger of a medic's practice. He might leave the station at 8:00 A.M. responding to a SIDS (sudden infant death syndrome) call. The family is hysterical, the infant is dead with rigor mortis already evident and there is not a thing the medic can do for the infant. Instead, the family becomes the patient and he must spend time counseling and consoling the parents. Sometimes, and this is an instantaneous judgment, if the family is disconsolate, it makes sense to work the infant, pretending that the child might be able to be revived. Some services teach their medics to whisk the child out to the ambulance, to begin CPR and other heroic but futile methods of resuscitation, continuing with the same all the way to the hospital. Under the theory that the parents are the patient at this point, this charade is meant to prove that everything possible was done and to somehow ease the pain of sudden, unexpected loss.

From the medic's point of view, this type of run is an absolute horror and takes time to work through. Then imagine that he's finished this run and is restocking the rig at the hospital. Five minutes later, he gets called to an auto accident where a news-paper vendor has been clipped by a commuter rushing to work. This one is easy; an open tib-fib fracture calls for splinting, pain management and transport. No big deal. An hour later he gets called to his five-year-old son's school, where an as yet unidenti-fied five-year-old male has fallen off the jungle gym and has a possible concussion. Now the stomach acids are really flowing. And so it goes throughout the day, with an occasional interruption for a snack on the run or a catnap in the recliner in front of a blaring TV at the station.

The ensuing emotional burnout is the single biggest danger of paramedicine. Once it happens, it can lead in several insidious direc-tions. Some medics become cynical way beyond their years; nothing is surprising, no human activity is unexpected. And cynicism in turn leads to depersonalization. People become patients who in turn are "that femur fracture" or the "CHF (congestive heart failure) over on Arlington Street." In the worst examples, depersonalization leads rapidly to impersonal, uncaring treatments, just going through the motions and following protocols without thought.

At other times, the stress and burnout become overwhelming. Drugs or alcohol become necessary props to get through the day or to get to sleep after a shift. Another path leads from depression to suicide, the ultimate way out of a depressing set of experiences.

More commonly than either of the above, experienced medics get run-down and worn-out. The initial enthusiasm gets buried under a sea of events and unimaginable injuries. For someone who honestly believed that he would spend his days saving lives, the encountered mix of irreversible injuries and illnesses is just too much. Thoughts turn to different lifestyles and other jobs that possibly earn more money.

A lot of every system's most promising medics get eaten by the very job they thought they would love and for which they worked so hard. And that is the real danger of the practice of paramedicine.

Abbreviations and Acronyms

ACLS advanced cardiac life support
AED automatic external defibrillator
AHA American Heart Association
ALI automated location identification
ALS advanced life support
AMS altered mental state (also ΔMS)
ANI automated number identification
ARDA American Rescue Dog Association
ATV all-terrain vehicle
BCD buoyancy control device
BLS basic life support
BSI body substance isolation
CAD computer-assisted dispatch
C/C chief complaint
CHEMTREC Chemical Transportation Emergency Center
CISD critical incident stress debriefing
CME continuning medical education
CNA certified nurse's aid
CPR cardiopulmonary resuscitation
D$_x$ diagnosis
E911 Enhanced 911 (also 911E)
ECG electrocardiogram (also EKG)
EMD emergency medical dispatch; emergency medical dispatcher
EMS emergency medical services
EMT emergency medical technician
EPA Environmental Protection Agency
EVOC Emergency Vehicle Operator Course

ff firefighter

FR first responder

FTD fixin' to die

FUNSAR "Fundamentals of Search and Rescue"

GPS global positioning systems

hazmat hazardous materials

helo helicopter

HPI history of present illness

H$_x$ patient history

IAFC International Association of Fire Chiefs

IAFF International Association of Firefighters

IAP incident action plan

IC incident commander

ICS Incident Command System

IDLH immediately dangerous to life and health

INSARTA International Search and Rescue Trade Association

IV intravenous

JEMS Journal of Emergency Medical Services

KED Kendrick Extrication Device

LAST Locate/Access/Stabilize/Treat

LKP last known place

LOC level of consciousness

LP lost person

MCI mass casualty incident

MDR mammalian diving reflex

MESAR Maine Search and Rescue

MOI mechanism of injury

MSDS Materials Safety Data Sheet

MVA motor vehicle accident

MVC motor vehicle crash

NASAR National Association for Search and Rescue

NCRC National Cave Rescue Commission

NFPA National Fire Protection Association

NG nitroglycerine

NRT National Response Teams

NSR normal sinus rhythm

N/V nausea and vomiting

Os oxygen
OSHA Occupational Safety and Health Administration
OTH over-the-hill
PA physician's assistant
PE physical exam
PEA pulseless electrical activity
PFD personal float devices
PI personal injuries
PLS point last seen
POA probability subject is within search area
POD probability of detection
POS probability of success
PPG personal protection gear
PSAPS Public Safety Access Points
QA quality assurance
SAR search and rescue
SCBA self-contained breathing apparatus
SCUBA self-contained underwater breathing apparatus
SIDS sudden infant death syndrome
SITSAT situation status
SOB shortness of breath
T$_x$ treatment
UAD up-and-die
USCG United States Coast Guard
V-fib ventricular fibrillation
WFR wilderness first responder (also "wofer")

Rescue Maladies

A Compendium of the Most Common Injuries and Illnesses

ABDOMINAL PAIN Distress in the region between the belly button (umbilicus) and the groin. The abdomen is divided into four visual quadrants, left/right and upper/lower.

ALTERED MENTAL STATE (ΔMS) Acting and talking differently than usual.

ANAPHYLAXIS A life-threatening allergic systemic problem (which means it affects the whole body), caused by, among others, bee stings, shellfish and medications.

BAROTRAUMA Damage to the body caused by extreme changes of pressure, whether the pressure was too low due to altitude or too high due to dive depths.

BURN Organ damage, especially to skin, caused by excessive heat due to fire, chemicals, radiation or electricity.

CARDIAC ARREST Sudden cessation of all effective pumping of the heart.

COLD CHALLENGE An attack by wind, temperature and moisture that drains body heat.

COMA A state of unconsciousness from which a patient cannot be aroused, even by powerful stimuli.

CYANOSIS Bluish tint to the skin caused by poor circulation and the relative absence of oxygen in the circulating blood.

DEHYDRATION A condition caused by losing too much body water due to sweating, vomiting or other causes.

DIABETES A disease caused by the body's inability to burn carbohydrates, which results in high blood sugar levels.

DROWNING Suffocation caused by either inhaling water (a wet drowning), or by a spasm of the throat that prevents water inhalation (a dry drowning).

DYSPNEA Difficult or labored breathing.

FOREIGN BODY OBSTRUCTION Partial or complete airway blockage caused by some object accidentally ingested.

FRACTURE A break as in bones. They are open or closed depending upon whether any bone fragments have pierced the skin.

HEAT EXHAUSTION Collapse caused by excessive loss of water and salt by sweating; characterized by cold, clammy skin and a rapid pulse. Leads to heat stroke, a dire emergency.

HEAT STROKE A life-threatening condition caused by disturbance to the body's temperature regulating mechanism; characterized by a fever, hot and dry skin, a bounding pulse and delirium or a coma.

HEMORRHAGE Uncontrolled bleeding, usually from an artery.

HYPERTHERMIA Abnormally high core body temperature.

HYPOTHERMIA Abnormally low core body temperature, below 90°F.

LACERATION A wound to the skin made by cutting or tearing.

PARALYSIS Loss of all motor function in an area of the body.

POISON Any agent that damages the body whether by inhalation, ingestion or contact.

PUNCTURE WOUND A wound to the skin caused by a sharp object entering the skin, such as a bullet or knife.

SHOCK A state of inadequate tissue oxygenation, caused by heart failure, excessive bleeding, nerve damage or any combination of the three. Not to be confused with surprise or fainting, incorrectly called shock.

SPRAIN Injury to the ligaments that connect bone to bone in a joint.

STRAIN Injury to the tendons that connect a joint/bone to muscle.

Alan Madison Productions. *Knots for Climbers, Cavers, S.W.A.T., Fire Rescue and Search and Rescue*. Fascinating video plus written guide on rescue-related knots.

———. *Swept Away . . . A Guide to Water Rescue Operations*. Rescue training video for those who respond to water emergencies.

American Academy of Orthopedic Surgeons. *Basic Rescue and Emergency Care*. 1990. Recommended medical treatments in the field.

———. *Rural Rescue and Emergency Care*. 1993. Practical instructions regarding hazmat, confined space, trench rescue, farm trauma.

American Canoe Association. *Heads Up! River Rescue for River Runners*. Video of real-life entrapments and rescue.

American Red Cross. *CPR for the Professional Rescuer*. 1993. Training manual for the professional rescuer's level of CPR

———. *Responding to Emergencies*. 1996. This first responder text covers all FR training requirements.

American Rescue Dog Association. *Search and Rescue Dogs: Training Methods*. 1991. Particular emphasis on unit training and obedience. Writers will be especially interested in chapters on how a dog's mind works and to what extent it can be trained.

Barsky, Steven M. *Diving in High Risk Environments*. 1990. A book describing the level of diving a professional rescuer would practice, yet explained in language that the neophyte would understand and find interesting.

———. *The Dry Suit Diving Manual*. 1990. Everything you need to know about dry suit diving.

Bechdel, Les and Slim Ray. *River Rescue*. Boston: Appalachian Mountain Club. 1985. The definitive guide to river rescue; old but still very useful.

Beck, Richard K. *Pharmacology for Prehospital Care*. 1992. Conveys an understanding of the drugs available to the paramedic.

Bledsoe, Bryan E., Robert Porter and Bruce R. Shade. *Paramedic Emergency Care*. 1994. Text including all skills and knowledge a medic must absorb.

Bownds, John M., Annita Harlan, David Lovelock and Charles McHugh. *Mountain Searches: Effectiveness of Helicopters*. 1991. Nine helo search scenarios are scrutinized.

Bronstein, Alvin C. and Phillip L. Currance. *Emergency Care for Hazardous Materials Exposure*. St. Louis: Mosby-Lifeline. 1994. A thorough guide to hazmat including explanation of the placard system, and signs, symptoms and treatment to hazmat-injured patients.

Brylske, Alex. *PADI Dive Rescue Manual*. Professional Association of Diving Instructors, Santa Ana, California. 1984. A somewhat dated but still very useful manual, heavily illustrated.

Bryson, Sandy. *Search Dog Training*. Boxwood Press, Pacific Grove, California. 1997. The bible on SAR dog handling. This is a training manual as well as general information on the techniques of training both the handler and the dog.

Button, Lue. *Practical Scent Dog Training*. 1990. A step-by-step guide for air scent training from the puppy on up.

Coonan, Patrick, Thomas J. Rahilly, Jonathan S. Rubens and Owen Traynor. *The Street Medic's Handbook*. Philadelphia: F.A. Davis. 1996. This streetwise guide reviews special situations, procedures and medico-legal documentation. The writer depicting a medic will find this helpful.

Cowan, James and Lois. *EMERGENCY RESCUE! Trouble at Moosehead Lake*. New York: Scholastic/Apple. 1993. Although children's reading, the five short stories include descriptions of shock, extrication, hazmat, anaphylaxis and search and rescue.

———. *EMERGENCY RESCUE! Nightmare at Norton's Mills*. New York: Scholastic/Apple. 1993. For readers ages eight to twelve, this volume includes stories with technical characterization of water rescue, winter rescue, paramedic response and search and rescue.

Downey, Ray. *The Rescue Company*. 1992. A chapter-by-chapter guide to all components of a successful rescue.

Fendler, Don as told to Joseph B. Egan. *Lost on a Mountain in Maine*. 1992. William Morrow. Originally published in 1939 and somewhat dated, this is the true story of a resourceful teenager who spent several weeks lost in the wilds of northern Maine. What is not dated are the passages that describe his dreams and fears as he confronts his aloneness as well as his hunger and cold.

Frank, James A. and Donald E. Patterson. *CMC Rappel Manual*. 1993. Rappel-based rescue operations and techniques.

Frank, James A. and Jerrold B. Smith. *CMC Rope Rescue Manual*. 1992. Standard text for rope rescuers. Clear and concise.

Goth, Peter and Jeff Isaac. *The Outward-Bound Wilderness First Aid Handbook*. New York: Lyons and Burford. 1991. An outstanding, medically accurate book about advanced care in the wilderness and elsewhere.

Hardy, Marian. *National Search and Rescue Dog Directory*. 1995. Practical information including call-out procedures for each unit, a glossary of terms, SAR dog team locations and SAR dog fact sheet.

Hudson, Steve and Tom Vines. *High-Angle Rescue Techniques*. 1992. A step-by-step primer for beginning rope rescuers.

The National Association of Search and Rescue. *Incident Commander Field Handbook: SAR*. Fairfax, VA. Undated. An all-weather flip book and a must for anyone wishing to write about SAR, this orange flip book will be in the hip pocket of every pro in the field. Includes charts, lists of probabilities and forms.

Jems Communications. *Rescue: The Magazine for Rescuers*. 1947 Camino Vida Roble, Suite 200, Carlsbad, CA 92008. Monthly magazine covering all rescue professions.

Koester, Robert J. *Wilderness and Rural Life Support Guidelines*. 1991. An illustrated, plastic-covered, pocket field guide for the professional medical provider on patient assessment, treatment for frostbite, hypothermia and other typical wilderness problems. Includes helo rescue, medications, CPR and burn tables.

Linton, Rust and Gilliam. *Dive Rescue Specialist: Training Manual*. Dive Rescue International, Fort Collins, Colorado. 1986. More heavily into urban problems in dive rescue such as search and vehicle extrication.

McClintock, James and Nancy Caroline. *Emergency Care in the Streets.* 1992. Text covering the practice of the highest level of EMT.

Morrissey, James. *The Wilderness Medical Associates' Field Guide.* A Guide for Wilderness Travelers, Outdoor Professionals and Rescue Specialists

NASAR. *Managing the Lost Person Incident (MLPI).* 1996. A loose-leaf book that is *the* text on SAR.

————. *Response: The Journal of the National Association for Search and Rescue.* NASAR, 4500 Southgate Place, Suite 100, Chantilly, VA 22021. (703) 222-NASR. Quarterly peer-reviewed journal.

National Cave Rescue Commission of the National Speleological Society. *Manual of Cave Rescue Techniques.* 1987. Definitive manual for the professional caver.

National Highway Traffic Safety Administration. *EMS Agenda for the Future.* 1996. Federal government spells out where EMS will be in the coming years.

Parr, Peggy. *Mountain High Mountain Rescue.* 1987. The adventure stories of western U.S. mountain teams.

Politano, Colleen. *Child Survival: Lost in the Woods.* 1984. A dramatic story for kids about a child's survival after being lost overnight. Porthole Press, Ltd. Sydney, British Columbia.

Ray, Slim. *Swiftwater Rescue.* CFS Press, Asheville, North Carolina. 1997. A long-awaited revision of the Bechdel and Ray volume of the same name, it illustrates the technology associated with swiftwater rescue and stresses the dangers associated with this form of rescue.

Roberts, Kathy. *Mounted Search and Rescue.* 1995. A manual for horseback SAR with an excellent glossary for the nonSAR-literate writer.

Roop, Michael, Richard Wright and Thomas Vines. *Confined Space and Industrial Rescue.* Mosby-Lifeline, St Louis, Missouri. 1997. This new text and study guide is the training standard of the profession.

Setnicka, Tim J. *Wilderness Search and Rescue.* Boston: Appalachian Mountain Club. 1980. Although it is not new, Setnika's 639-page tome continues to be the best manual for the wilderness rescuer. If an author is planning to buy one rescue book, this is it.

Smith, Barry. *Rescuers in Action*. Mosby-Lifeline, St. Louis, Missouri. 1996. A large-format picture book with over three hundred action-packed photos depicting fire, mountain and swiftwater rescue and aircraft environments and efforts. Helpful for describing gear and uniforms.

Smith, Daniel I., editor. *The Handbook of Cave Rescue Operations*. National Cave Rescue Commission, Huntsville, Alabama. Undated. As its name implies, this book will guide the writer through a full description of a cave rescue from the rescuers' point of view.

Smith, David S. and Sara J. *Water Rescue: Basic Skills for Emergency Responders*. 1994. Text focusing on realistic, dangerous rescue locations; flood rescue planning is included.

Syrotuck, William G. *Scent and the Scenting Dog*. 1972. The book on a dog's ability to perceive a human's presence and to discriminate one human from another.

———. *Introduction to Land Search Probabilities*. 1975. Theoretical mathematical probability applied to lost person behavior.

———. *Analysis of Lost Person Behavior*. 1977. A fascinating examination of 229 search incidents.

United States Fire Administration. *Technical Rescue Technology Assessment*. Federal Emergency Management Agency; FA-153, 1/95. A comprehensive review and description of all rescue equipment including glances into the future. With photos.

Walbridge and Sundmacher. *Whitewater Rescue Manual: New Techniques for Canoeists, Kayakers, and Rafters*. Techniques for self-rescue of companions on the river. Includes exciting case histories as sidebars.

Work, Kathy, R.N. with Jon Kushner, EMT-P. *MedDive Manual*. 1991. A comprehensive guide for in-the-field treatment of diving injuries.

Environmental Protection Agency (EPA),
hazmat response guidelines, 97
EPA. *See* Environmental Protection
Agency
Epilepsy, 218
Epinephrine, 216
Equipment
cave rescuer, 159-160
dispatcher, 24-25
dog handler, 49-50
emergency medical technician,
203-206
extrication specialist, 90-93
firefighter, 74-77
hazmat rescuer, 103-105
paramedic, 216-218
ranger, 62-63
rope rescuer, 139-140
search-and-rescue team, 173-175
water rescuer, 124-127
winter rescuer, 147-151
EVOC. *See* Emergency Vehicle Operator
Course
Exposure, route of, 105
Extrication specialist, 3, 81-94
dangers, 93-94
education and certification, 85-86
equipment, 90-93
history of profession, 81-85
job description, 86-90
language, 93

Fern snow, 152
Fire department
collapse rescue, 84
rope rescue, 136
today's, 68-69
trench rescue, 85
vehicle rescue, 83
See also Firefighter
Firefighter, 3, 66-80
cross-training, 68-70
dangers, 78-79
education and certification, 69-73
equipment, 74-75
first responders, 74
as hazmat responder, 97
history of profession, 68-69
job description, 73-74

language, 75, 78
as paramedics, 6
physical monitoring, 79
qualifications, 73
as searchers, 32
Firefighter Combat Challenge, 71
Fire rehab, 79
Fire Rescue magazine, 86, 106
First responder (FR), 6, 180-192
dangers, 191-192
dog handler as, 47
education and certification, 184-185
equipment, 189-190
history of profession, 180-184
job description, 185-189
language, 190-191
qualifications, 185
Flashover, 78
Foreign body obstruction, 230
Fracture, 230
Franklin, Ben, 68
Free falls, 137
"Fundamentals of Search and Rescue"
(FUNSAR), 2, 165
Funeral home ambulance, 194-195
FUNSAR, 2, 165
Furosemide, 217

Glacier, wet, 153
Global positioning system (GPS), 110,
173
Glucagon, 217
Grains, 152
Great St. Bernard's Hospice, 163
Grid search, 165, 170, 172
Guiding, backcountry, 56

Hal Foss Award, 167
Handbook of Cave Rescue Operations, The,
155
Handler, 50
See also Dog handler
Harness, 141
Hasty team, 57, 63
Haystacks, 129
Hazardous material, 4
defined, 96
See also Hazmat
Hazardous materials rescue, 95